# *LITTLE* **BOBBY REESE**
## GROWING UP IN EXTON PA

BY
ROBERT REESE

***Little Bobby Reese***
***Growing Up in Exton, PA***
by Robert Reese


Copyright © 2015


All rights reserved.


Library of Congress Number: 2015903814
International Standard Book Number: 978-1-60126-449-7

*Printed 2015 by*
Masthof Press
*219 Mill Road*
*Morgantown, PA 19543-9516*

# TABLE OF CONTENTS

Foreword .......................................... v

Map of Exton in 1930s ................... vi

The 1930s ........................................ 1

The 1940s ...................................... 14

The 1950s ...................................... 29

The 1960s ...................................... 55

The 1970s .................................... 108

The 1980s .................................... 133

The 1990s & 2000s .................... 144

## FOREWORD

This is the story of my life growing up in Exton, Pennsylvania, from 1931 until now, 2010. These are my memories of how Exton grew from a tiny village into a thriving town in the middle of Chester County, Pennsylvania. This book will be of history, goodwill, adventure and anecdotes of life in a small village.

CREDIT
Writer-Robert Reese
Editors- Elizabeth Dougherty and Jeremy Tucker
Photos-Dorothy Funderwhite, Morris Lasada and Sharon L. Williams
Story Credits-Willie K.E. Weichelt, VMD
Rodger Steward of Jimmy Johns Hot Dogs

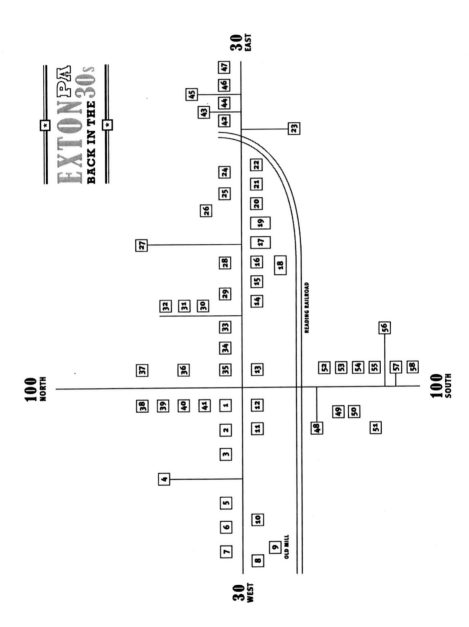

| # | | # | |
|---|---|---|---|
| 1 | Worrell Garage and Gas Station | 20 | Rodney's Fruit Market |
| 2 | Mr. Darlington's Real Estate and Notary | 21 | Rodney's General Store |
| 3 | Morris Seeds –(later was Justice of the Peace) | 22 | Dutt's Home |
| 4 | The Meades | 23 | Massey's Home |
| 5 | Dick Thomas | 24 | Paterson's Home |
| 6 | Gusatson | 25 | Trego's Home |
| 7 | Chandlers | 26 | Garage and Blacksmith Shop |
| 8 | The Brick Oven or Dick Thomas's | 27 | Trimble's Home |
| 9 | Old Water Wheel and Grinding Mill | 28 | George Bair (Tax Collector) |
| 10 | Hagee's | 29 | House's Home |
| 11 | Exton Lodge (Owner, John Hatton) | 30 | John Loftus |
| 12 | Texaco Gas Station | 31 | Bill Loftus (House's tenants) |
| 13 | Valley Creek Coffee House – Restaurant, Gas Station, and Post Office | 32 | The Forest Family |
| | | 33 | The Cow |
| 14 | Chester Fetter's Home | 34 | Larry Polite's Home |
| 15 | Charlie Wells' Home | 35 | Sunoco Gas Station |
| 16 | Henry Smith Rental | 36 | Lockwood Estate |
| 17 | Henry Smith's Garage and Gas Station | 37 | Ashbridge |
| 18 | Wayne Delaney's Feed Mill | 38 | Ashbridge |
| 19 | Wayne Delaney's Feed Mill | 39 | Howard Trego |
| 40 | Normal Worrell's Home |
| 41 | Exton Diner |
| 42 | Mom Dean's Hotel |
| 43 | The Messner's Home |
| 44 | Williams' Motel Restaurant and Gas Pumps |
| 45 | Williams' Home |
| 46 | Amoco Bulk Plant |
| 47 | Atlantic Bulk Plant |
| 48 | Newlin Estate |
| 49 | Newlin Garage and Barn |
| 50 | Barn |
| 51 | Habard's Home (Newl n Estate) |
| 52 | George Robert's Home |
| 53 | Elwood Erwin Home |
| 54 | John Rise |
| 55 | Barney Rodewalt |
| 56 | Mike Mallack |
| 57 | Russell Brumgard |
| 58 | Horace Collin |

## The 1930s

In the early 1930s, Dad and Mom owned and operated a restaurant and gas station at the corner of Route 30 and Route 100 in Exton, PA. Both roads had two lanes, each with a stop sign on Route 100. Also located by our place was a one-lane bridge. Just past the bridge was one of the steepest hills around—so steep coal trucks had trouble climbing the hill. The restaurant was called the Valley Creek Coffee House.

In 1936, my mom took over the post office, which had been in Rodney's Store just down the road from our place. It

*Valley Creek, 1935*

was an eight-class post office back then. The rent for having a post office in our place? Whatever the stamp sales were—$400 for the whole year!

In the early 1930s, the population in West Whiteland Township was about 200—there were more cows than people!

Days started early for our family. Mom got up before sunrise to bake bread and forty pies for the restaurant. We had seven girls working back then. We specialized in chicken and waffles—it was all you could eat for $.35. Was that a deal, or what? She also cooked and picked 300 chickens a week for the chicken and waffles.

I, Bobby Reese, was born in 1931 and I can remember events from 1936 on up until now, when I am writing this book (2009-2011, 2012-13).

In the late 1800s, Grandfather Reese owned a 700-acre farm, which is now part of Church Farm School. He also owned what was at the time called the Ship Inn Tea Room, which later became the Ship Inn.

*Coffee House Restaurant, 1920*

My father in the early 1920s had a garage and blacksmith shop on Route 30.

Grandfather owned the coffee shop until the early 1920s, when dad took over. Dad also had a farm on Route 401 just past Ludwig's Corner. We had twenty-six cows on the farm, along with geese, ducks and chickens.

At the time, Exton was a small village with seven gas stations, our restaurant and the Gurney Cow, Dick Thomas', Exton Lodge, Mom Dean's Beer Joint, plus William's Motel and Eating Place.

During wintertime in the early 1930s we would go sledding down Robert's Hill behind us and across the railroad tracks. There was a pond across from us on Exton Lodge's place where we used to go ice skating. I remember we always had my friend Elwood try out the ice first. If he didn't fall through, it was safe to skate on! I never skated—I would just run and slide on the ice.

In the late 1930s, my oldest brother Clyde and I used to trap up and down the creek that was behind our place. We would trap for weasels, and now and then we would have a skunk in the trap. One time I didn't want to go to school, so I let the skunk pee on me. We went to a one-room school back then and when I opened the door, the teacher said, "Out!!" I got to go home, where I got a whipping for letting the skunk get me.

I was always getting into something, even when I was little. I was always doing something to get in trouble with Mom. One time when I was five, we had a back area that served as our living room. We had the restaurant, which was the main part of the building, and our bedrooms were upstairs. This room was behind the kitchen, where I would play with my toys. I loved my cast-iron fire trucks. Every once in a while, a state cop used to stop by. So this one day he decided to tease me, but he didn't know I had a temper. He picked up all my fire trucks and said he was going to take them with him. I went to the corner and got my baseball bat, got up on a chair, and hit him alongside his head—and down he went—out cold! Dad came back and got some salts to bring him to. Dad apologized to him, but he said, "Mr. Reese, I didn't know he had a temper. If so, I wouldn't have done that to him. I am sorry."

I remembered his name, which I won't say, for one day many years later I was next door, which was across the railroad tracks. Morris Seeds was District Judge and a personal friend of mine. He said, "I want you to meet so and so." I looked at him and said, "Does your head hurt you at times?" And he looked at me and said, "Matter of fact, it does." I said "I was that kid that hit you with my baseball bat." He laughed, and we shook hands and put it behind us.

Getting back to my early years, we had the restaurant, post office, and gas pumps. I remember in 1937 we had gas wars. There were seven gas stations in Exton, and Dad went and talked to everybody about not getting into a gas war that year. In the 30s we were pumping 30,000 gallons a month, which is small compared to what stations pump today. Gas was $.14 a gallon back then. Come Memorial Day, they would drop the price to $.12, but Dad talked them into not dropping the price.

So the day came that someone pulled up to the pumps and looked at our price, and said, "You are higher than across the road." Dad got in his car and drove around to everybody and told them if they didn't go back up, he would go down and stay down all summer.

They didn't listen, so Dad said paint the signs, and we went down to $.10 a gallon, and stayed there all summer. Our station became so popular that we were running out of gas, so Dad ordered more. We sold Atlantic gas, and the bulk plant was in Exton. The company told us they wouldn't sell us any more gas until we raised the price. Dad told them to deliver the gas that night or their pumps would be sitting by the road in the morning, for we owned the tanks in the ground. They delivered that night, and we kept the price at $.10 all summer! We were the only ones in Exton that stayed open all night for gas. We had a room at the corner of the store that was open where Austin Fowler stayed and pumped gas. Back in the day, there were a lot of coal trucks that used to stop.

In the 1930s, Dad had some of the tables set up with checkers for the farmers to sit and have coffee and wait for the milk trucks to pick up the milk. We could seat about seventy people. We had more cows than people back then. Also, I guess we were different than some. Mom and Dad had one rule: Their rule was that everybody who walked into our place was to behave themselves. Have fun but don't cause trouble. We did not care what color you were. We served everybody, even if you had little or no money we would give you a meal. Ask us for anything and we would help. But don't try to steal. Our police dogs wouldn't let that happen.

One night about 11:00, a man walked in and pointed a gun at my dad, not knowing one dog was behind the counter. The dog cleared the counter and crushed the guy's hand and about that time we heard a noise out back. We went out back and there was the other dog with a man by his throat and wouldn't let go until we got there. Our dogs were German

Sheppards brought over from Germany by my grandfather. They each weighed 170 pounds. Not many people fooled with them.

In the late 30s, Dad bought chickens and I raised them for eggs. I had close to 150 laying hens. I would collect the eggs and sell what mom didn't need. Back then I got $.65 a dozen and I'll never forget I paid $2.78 for 100 pounds. Hens lay more today and the price is a lot higher.

At the restaurant, Dad and Mom did the cooking, and Clyde and Herb worked in the kitchen washing dishes and making pepper cabbage and coleslaw. Earl worked the gas pumps during the day after school, and on Saturdays and Sundays. I worked the soda fountain and the register. I used to have my baseball bat in the corner, in case somebody got rowdy. I used it a few times. Besides taking care of my chickens, I tended the coal furnace over at the Exton Lodge for Mr. Hatton.

We had a two-story, two-car garage with second floor and we built a porch and enclosed it with wire, so the chickens could get outside. One morning as I was going up the stairs, I saw a rat trying to get at the feed. I grabbed a bat I had there and went after the rat. Next thing I knew, it went inside my pant leg and bit me. That made me mad. I grabbed it by the tail and pulled it out, then grabbed it by the neck and squeezed it until its eyes popped. I went ahead and fed the chickens, calmed them down, gathered the eggs, then went to the house.

Mom looked at me and asked what was wrong. I told her a rat bit me. She said, "Get your coat, we're going to Doc Mercer," who was in Downingtown, "to get a shot."

All we had at the crossroads those days was a stop sign on Route 100, but people didn't always stop, so we had one or two accidents every week. We had trucks loaded with eggs come through the front corner of the building—eggs all over the place!

Tony Landers was what we called a keystone cop. He was constable at the time. He would be in the middle of the crossroads directing traffic on Sundays. Back in the early days, cars weren't fast like today.

In the wintertime we got a lot of snow, and all we had in those days were big graders. On Route 100 past our place going south was a one-way bridge, and it had a big bump. If you went too fast, you'd plane and bottom out when you hit the other side. Then there was the hill. It was not big, but it was about the steepest little hill around.

With the snow in the wintertime, the coal trucks couldn't get up the hill. Smitty from Smitty's Garage on Route 30 would chain his tow truck to a big tree God put there for that purpose. Then he would hook up his cable and winch the coal trucks up the hill. Sometimes he was there half the night. All the truckers were always overloaded—that was why they couldn't make the hill. I still talk about that hill to a few fellows down where I live now, who used to stop at our place and get gas. By the way, today as I write this story, it is a six-lane highway with turn lanes. There were at least a couple accidents every week at the crossroads. Different times there were trucks hauling steel out of Lukens Steel that would pile up in the crossroads. I knew when the steel trucks would crash. The steel let loose and would crush the cab of the truck and be fatal.

We had a trash pile out back across the creek where we burned everything. I remember one night I had carried trash out and set fire to the pile then went back inside and Dad was looking for a brown paper bag. He asked me if I had seen it. I said, "No, why?" He said it had money in it. We ran out to the fire and started to spread the trash around, and we found the bag by luck.

Back in the school days in the 1930s, the school was a two-story building with the first floor housing grades one through six. The second floor was for 7th and 8th grades. There were four schools in the township: Ship Road, Whitford, Grove, and Greenwood. Three schools had 1st through 6th grades, and 7th and 8th grades all went to Ship Road School.

In our days growing up, we didn't have any problems with color or race. We played together as neighbors and helped one another back then. We had two quarry holes behind the school, and we would play in them sometimes. At recess, we played baseball and in the wintertime we played football. We found fence rails and built a boxing ring. We got in the ring and boxed. We also played baseball. That was the biggest sport back then. I remember Clarence Johnson and myself would get to fighting at recess. I don't know, it was just a boy thing I guess. I remember one time I was chasing Clarence through where they were playing ball, and was running through as a boy was swinging a bat, and he hit me right on the nose, and I just kept on going. They said, "He has a hard head!" What makes me laugh as I look back on my school days is looking at my handwriting now—back then I used to take all the penmanship ribbons in my class! Even though I was getting into trouble, I had good grades.

Life back in the 1930s was a simpler time. We went to school, came home, did homework, then had things to do around the house or worked in the store. Back then, there wasn't much to do besides work and play baseball. It's not like today, with all the toys and gadgets to play with. We would go to the town of West Chester on a Saturday night. After we finished the shopping for the week, we got to go to the movies. Back then it cost $.10—a far cry from today's prices. Besides the store, post office, and restaurant, we also grew strawberries, potatoes, and tomatoes. We got paid $.03 per quart of berries, $.10 for a 5/8 basket of tomatoes, and $.15 for a 5/8 basket of potatoes. I hated picking potatoes! We used a single-row potato plow to dig, and I had to ride the mule bareback. We had ten acres of potatoes. Once, a snake was in the row, and the mule got scared and threw me off and ran—breaking the plow loose and taking off. We found him about a mile away, and came back to finish plowing the potatoes. After being dug, we had to get down and crawl along the rows with a bag with straps around our necks. We had to pick it full and dump the potatoes in baskets.

Tomatoes we would pick back all ripe. It is not like today, where in the big fields they check the field and when they see 50% ripe they spray the rest so they turn red, then spray to kill the vines. Then they pick them with machines. Back in our day, we would pick to make the basket level, then they were stacked on trucks in rack fashion and hauled to the cannery. They couldn't haul them that way today—first curve they would be all over the road. Strawberries we picked by the quart at $.03, and you better not have a bad one in it!

I would get up in the morning in the winter, get breakfast, then head to the Exton Lodge to stoke the coal furnace and take out the ashes. Then I had to care of my chickens. I would bring in the eggs, check them with a bright light for blood, then box them for sale. I would get $.65 per dozen for my eggs back then.

In the summertime I would work in the fields a few hours, then work in the store behind the counter dipping ice cream or making sundaes. We only had a store in those days. If you wanted a pint or a quart, we had to dip it for you. We used to sell about a thousand gallons of ice cream a week. This was because we sold so much chicken and waffles in the day. Chicken and waffles were big in our day. It was all you could eat for $.35! We bought our waffle mix in 100-pound tins back then. We also had steaks and seafood. Speaking of seafood, every Friday night we would have shad, and it had all kinds of bones in it.

Back in the late 30s, Exton had a baseball team. They started to play across the road behind what was John Hatton's Exton Lodge. Then they moved across to our own back field where we had raised tomatoes and potatoes for market.

By 1939 we stopped growing in the back field, and we turned it into a baseball diamond. When we got done raking out the stones, we had an old '32 Chevy and scraper that we used to scrape the infield. It turned out that we had the best infield in the county. Dad managed the ball team, and I was the bat boy for years. Clyde and Earl played, and there were, as I can remember, Bob Parke, Dick Sload, Bob and Bill Parry, Charlie and Harry Clouser, Elwood Berengard, Harry Trego, Charlie Schriner, Chick Messner, and others that I cannot remember, and I am sorry for that.

I forget how many teams there were, but they had a league even back then. I remember West Chester had a team called Dean Street. Paoli, Berwyn, Downingtown, DeVault, and Kimberton all had teams. There were a couple more that I do not remember. They all played up until the war started, and then at that time most of the men went into the service.

---

I remember my days as a boy: I had a row boat, and at night I would row all the way to Whitford Road and back home. The creek behind our place was three feet deep in the 30s. Look at it now—you can walk across it and not get wet!

I would fish in the creek, for it was clean in our day. I liked pulling trout out and taking them home, cleaning and cooking and eating them right away. That's good eating!

In 1939 Harold Martin bought the Exton Lodge, and I still stoked the furnace for him for years. Back in those days, a lot of places burned trash and garbage, but we had a field for that. We composted our garbage, and when it was ready, used it in the garden. We still had a big garden.

Mom always canned every year. I can still taste Mom's pickles she put up—It was always the right vinegar mixture. She used to get homemade vinegar from Mrs. Messner, but you had to cut it. It was that strong! She made it in 55-gallon wood barrels.

Mrs. Messner's daughter, Helen, worked for us at the restaurant back in the 30s. There was also, Mary Trego, Olive Trego, Mim Smith, Clair Rimel, and three others (I forget their names). They worked, I believe, upwards of 10 to 12 hours back then. Nobody today knows what it was like back then. In the early 30s, everybody had it hard, but when we could we would help people. If people needed supplies or food, our door was open to help. Many times people would come in and had no money, but they could set down and eat. We weren't wealthy, but we made out.

Somehow, I always managed to get in trouble before the day was over. Mom would beat me just about every day, and if she didn't, I'd say, "Mom, are you sick today?" and then I would get in spades. Even though I was bad, I didn't do bad things like some kids do today, just little things that made Mom mad, and then I would get it.

I always was smart in school and was on the Honor Roll all the way up to 12$^{th}$ grade. Then I hit a bump in the road. I'll get to that later.

Baseball was our pastime, and also on Saturday nights we'd go to our neighbor's house, Mr. Fetters. He had clay quay pits with lights so we could play at night. After some time of pitching quays, we got pretty good—so good that we only counted ringers. Sometimes Herb, my brother, and I would pitch against one another, and we would put all four quays on the pick for four ringers.

We would play cards at night during the wintertime when we were not busy. Only played 500. I would look in my opponents' glasses and read their cards, then after some time Mom said, "How can you know what I have?" Then I told her I could read them in her glasses, and man, did she get mad at me! When they found out I could see their cards, they all sat back so I couldn't see their cards. Mom finally got over it, but didn't forget it.

Looking back over the years I cannot remember ever having a birthday cake. Sad, I guess, but we were glad to have a roof over our heads and food on the table. Younger people have no idea what it was like back then. If you got a couple of toys for Christmas you were lucky. But one thing we did have was a family that stayed together. We had our moments. My brother, Earl, liked to pick on me and try to make me do things to get into trouble with Mom. Back then we really didn't have much fun time. We had to pull our weight around the house and our Dad had a farm that we also worked on. I milked cows, and walked behind plows with horses and mules. I was 14 years old when I had a mule kick me in the head. Some say that's why I am crazy and bad! I was so mad you won't believe what I did. I took the mule by his ears and head-butted him. I had a hard head, believe me! Two of my friends watched, and if they hadn't seen it, they wouldn't have believed it. The mule never did that again! When I would hitch him to the plow, there was no more trouble!

*Bob Reese, 1942*

# The 1940s

Now we are going into the 1940s and the war years. I remember Pearl Harbor, and soon after that everyone pitched in to help in one way or another. By now we just had the restaurant, gas station, and post office, and I remember in the early 40s I joined the boy scouts, and we went out to collect paper and scrap iron for the war effort.

> I believe it was 1944, the war was heating up on both fronts, and some of us not being old enough still snuck off to join the army, but they sent us home to work on the farms.
>
> This will be hard for a lot of people to believe, but it is true. Four of us decided to take a steer after it was born, which it would weigh 70 pounds, and lift it over our heads twice a day. After several months of picking up the steers, I was able to lift 525 pounds over my head. Dick Swanenberg went to 531 pounds and beat me. This is a true story, and not many kids messed with us, at least not the second time around.

Our life during the war years wasn't very exciting, to say the least. We all worked and pulled together in the effort of the war.

*Lettie, Clyde, and Clyde, Jr. Reese, 1942*

*Herb, Clyde and Bob, 1940*

*Earl, Clyde, Bob and Lettie Reese, 1942*

*Bob Reese, bat boy, 1939*

*Bob Reese, 1939*

We still went to school and when we got home our day changed. We had to work in the store until we closed, then at night do our homework. There was no time to play. The women would knit squares and make blankets for the servicemen. Even we helped to knit squares for the blankets. I made close to 300 squares myself, for this was what you did to help out.

During the war, we had rationing of gasoline and food, but we endured. That's what made America the greatest nation in the world, for we, the people, pulled together and got the job done. The younger people will probably never realize what it took to make this country the greatest, and we were a proud people for what we had done. No nation could come together and do what the old people had done. Back in our day everybody worked, and they learned how to work.

---

In 1945 after the war and Clyde and Earl came home, Mom and Dad set us down one night and we talked about the restaurant. They asked us if we wanted to carry on with it, but being we all worked in the store, we said no. Down the road, we wished we had said yes. Atlantic Refinery Co. wanted to buy the corner, so Dad sold a 100 x 100 piece to them and got ready to move the building. John Deere from Philadelphia came out and moved the building across the creek to where it set for years. We redid the outside of the building. We still had the post office there until the 1960s when we got a new post office.

It was spring of 1945 and we were playing football. One of the fellows tackled me, and I hit a bridge wall. When I got up, I couldn't walk. They took me to the hospital, and Doc Barker put my legs back in place and put a cast on.

In 1945, I guess in May or June, we moved back to the house back across the creek. When we were on the corner all those years, the noise of Lenard H. Hines trucks leaving at 3:00 and 4:00 o'clock in the morning never bothered us. But when we moved across the creek and set up, we couldn't sleep, for there was no noise. Crazy, but true.

In 1946 Joe Mentt and Domick Oilpotti had the diner across the corner from us. Ottio Linton and his partner opened up Speedcraft Auto Shop. They repaired and built cars. This was in Lenard Hines' building alongside the Old Orchard Restaurant and Dance Hall.

---

In the summertime, after school and Saturdays, I mowed seven lawns in my *spare* time. It was a total of 13 acres of grass, and I used a push-behind reel mower. I got my exercise back then!

I was able to have the time to row our boat down the creek all the way to Whitford Road. It was quiet and peaceful. Baseball was our big sport in those days; then came football in the fall and winter.

Always on Thanksgiving, there was at least a foot of snow on the ground for the football games. West Chester and Berwyn were rivals.

Like I said, back in the 1940s there wasn't much else besides working, going to school, playing ball, and doing boy scout things. We got to go camping on weekends, and that taught us a lot about campfires and cooking out in the open. Over the next three years I got all my merit badges but one, and that was lifesaving. In 1945, we were playing sandlot football, and I got knocked against a bridge wall and knocked my hip out. I laid in a cast for 18 weeks, and had to drink 2 quarts of goat milk a day. Goat's milk grows calcium twice as fast as cow's milk.

I was one merit badge from being an Eagle Scout. They wanted to give me a substitute, but I wouldn't take it. I wish I had now, because scouting meant a lot to me. I have always been a good boy scout, even to this day, which is now February 2014. I always went out of my way to help people all the time. I would shovel snow for the older people or mow their lawns and not take any money.

---

## 1946-47

Scouting back in our day was a lot different than today. We had our meetings every Monday night at the school. Our scouting days were in the Second World War. We were active in the war effort. We went around collecting iron and paper for the war effort. We also always helped people in the area with whatever was needed. It made us feel good about ourselves and made us better people.

I will always remember Mr. Daily and his son Dave. They helped out and took us on camping trips. We had weekends with all the troops in the county at Longwood.

I will never forget when we were there this one time. We had a bow and arrow show. Andy Smith was our scout leader and he was a bow and arrow expert, so to speak, and he taught us how to shoot. We got so good at the show, Andy put five arrows in the bull's eye and guess what? I split his arrows. He said, "I guess I taught you too good!"

---

In late 1945, after I was out and about and back in shape, I started playing baseball and I got real good at it. We had formed a league. There was Exton, Frazer, Malvern, West Chester, Downingtown, Glenmoore, Guthriesville, and Lionville. I was (and always will be) a left-hander, and I had a good eye at the bat. I also had a knack for hitting the ball past players when they moved out of place. I carried a .500 batting average most of the time. I could hit to any field, but I never hit a home run. I had a lot of singles, doubles, and walks. In 1947, my brother, Clyde, and I played some pro ball. We got $18.00 per game back then. Ray Beam and I played ball on the same team in 1947. Ray worked for Rubinstein's in West Chester for 70 years and is now 90. I played up until about 1951 or 1952. I think it was 1949 when we played the state champion American Legion at our field. I was up to bat, and the third baseman moved over toward the bag, and the coach said, "He's left-handed. Get off the bag." The boy had played against me before, so he knew what I could do. He said, "If I move, he'll hit it right over the bag." But he moved over. I said to the catcher, who was Eslie Chandler, who I went to high school with, "I am going to waste a pitch." I turned as the ball came in, and hit the ball at the bench where the coach was sitting, and he fell back off the bench. Then the next pitch I hit right over the third base bag.

I went on to hit five for five that night, and there were scouts from the big leagues there: The Brooklyn Dodgers signed Bob Ludwich that night. He was the league pitcher. They came over to me. They said, "You swing at a lot of bad pitches, but we've never seen anybody hit to all fields before like you do." A couple of teams wanted to give me a tryout, but a fellow walked up behind them and said, "He has a bad hip," and they were gone. I just played a few years after that.

In 1946, '47, and '48, I used to go up to Worthington's Orchard and pick peaches, then apples. I did that for two summers, and in the winter, at Thanksgiving, I worked at McIlvaine's killing turkeys. I killed 500 turkeys a day. Back then, you would string them up and slit their throats. I also helped out at Christmas.

In 1945, I believe, Clyde and Violet got married, and they bought a house up in Thorndale on the hill. We all helped to do some fixing up on the house. That was back in the days when everybody helped as a family, which I always thought was a good thing. After Clyde came Earl's Caroline in 1946. For them we built a new house from the cellar up. I forget how long it took to build, but we had it finished by the time they got married. I remember walking the ridgepole again, and nailing rafters. I remember one day we were putting on the storm windows. Dad went around the corner and a wind came up so Dad had to run and turn the window so as not to lose it. A while back when Dad was cutting the rafters, you had to check to see if the rafter had a belly. If it did, you turned that side down before you cut the rafter.

Dad was looking down one board, while Caroline was walking past, and Dad said, "Look at the belly on that!" He meant the board, but Caroline told Earl, "Your father is being fresh!" We all laughed at that, and Earl told her he was looking at the board, not her.

In the summer of 1947 my brother, Clyde, worked for John Fisher, who was a contractor. Mr. Fisher had the contract to fix all county bridges, which took in covered bridges.

We also worked on the old schools that were built back in the day. They had 18-inch walls, and after you had a hole in the wall, it was sand, and the stone would fall out. Then there was a lot of rebuilding to do.

We were working on a bridge over by the quarry north of Paoli. It was summertime and I was on a sling under the bridge, and it was hot! Somebody cut one of the ropes, and down into the water I went. It felt good, but took a while to dry out.

We worked on a lot of the old churches that had slate roofs. We would tie off ropes so that you wouldn't fall if a slate broke under you. We built stick houses back in the 40s. I'll never forget, they put me up on the ridgepole, which was a 2x6, and I walked that and would lean over and nail in the rafters. I look back on those days and say, "I couldn't do that today! I am going on 83 next month!"

On the weekends, Morris Seeds, who lived across the road on Route 30, had built carts and sold peanuts. We had moved our building off the corner back in 1945, so I sat on our corner on Saturdays and Sundays selling peanuts. I always kept busy doing something to make money or helping somebody out. I never went out with a girl until I was 19 years old. I worked all the time. I had a couple of girls ask me to go to the prom, but I said, "I don't dance, and I don't have time anyway."

Speaking of dancing, I forgot to tell you about a place called the old Orchard Dance Hall and eating place, down on Route 30 from our place, which was on the southeast corner of Exton Crossroads. They had the old-time square dance there. Krapf owned the place back then.

Sometimes on the weekends we would get to go camping out in the woods, or we would go to Camp Horseshoe, which consisted of 700 acres, including winter cabins, summer cabins, a mess hall, and a community center. We enjoyed going there. We had things to do like hiking, swimming, and we used to always have a project to make the place better when we left. We had plenty of deer all year round, and back then they would walk right up and eat out of your hands.

Sometime in 1948 I became a patrol leader and started a patrol in Lionville. Some of the fellows I had with me were George and Merrit Ruark, Carl Ruth, Dick Ruth, Don Ferrell, and others. It makes you feel good when the fellows come back years later and tell you that you helped them learn about life and God. That's what makes helping people worth it. Scouting is one of the best things a young fellow can do. It gives you a sense of being, and it has great rewards. I am, even to this day (getting ready to turn 83 in March), proud of being a boy scout.

In the summer of 1948, I went to work with John Fisher again, with my brother. We were putting on a roof in the north end of Coatesville, on Route 82. The road was at the edge of the house, so our ladders were on the road. It was a three-story house, and steep, so we had to nail boards down to walk and stay up. One broke as I was on the way down. My brother was coming up the ladder, caught me by my belt, and got me back on the roof and I kept on working. Another guy said if that would have been him, he would have quit for the day. I said, "All in a day's work."

One morning in 1949 as we were riding the bus to school it was so foggy that you couldn't see 10 feet in front of the bus. We got to Whitford Road and needed to turn off Route 30; the driver turned and a car hit the bus under the gas tank. The driver was knocked out and the girls were scared. We went to open the back door, but it was jammed shut. I told Dick Sawenberg to push down the handles, and I hit the door, and it opened. We hurried to get the girls off, then went and got the driver out, for a fire was burning in the front of the bus. After that day, whenever we got to school, the boys went out the back door to make sure it would open. One day a cop got on the bus, let the girls get off, then came back and told us not to use the back door. I said, "We want to make sure that it opens, after that accident." He didn't seem to care about that. What he didn't know was that most of the boys were farm boys. He made me mad so I told one boy to open the door and I took the cop and put him out the back door, then jumped down and wanted to know what he was going to do. He said, "You made your point. Let's be friends." One lesson here is that city boys don't want to mess with farm boys.

In 1949, I graduated from West Chester High School. I believe we were the last or next to last class to graduate from West Chester High. The senior high school burned down at Christmas in 1947. I was in the woodshop and Mr. Musselman was our teacher. The new school was going to be built where there was a nursery. The boys in the shop had to go over and help clear out the nursery. We took down the fence that was around the grounds. I was using a big wire cutter. Not watching the handle, I got my finger in between the handle and mashed my little finger.

Mr. Musselman took me to Chester County Hospital. There the doctor took my finger and was hurting me, so I said, "Doc, it hurts enough without you hurting it more." He said, "You hurt, you suffer." With that said, I up and hit him and drove him through a partition that was being used as a temporary wall. Somebody called security and two guards came charging at me, and I drove them through the partition, too.

Mr. Musselman said, "We better get out of here!" He took me to West Chester Memorial, which is now Paoli Hospital.

I enjoyed being in the wood shop. I made bookends, some tables, and used to love making things with the lathe.

When we got our graduation pictures taken, I have to look back and laugh at myself. For when we went to see our proofs, I was walking toward the door and looking at my proof, and said, "This is not my picture." I went back to the lady, and she looked at my picture, then at me, and said, "It is you." My buddies looked and laughed and said, "Bob, it is you." And I said, "Am I that ugly?" and we all laughed.

The prom was coming up, and somebody said, "Are you going?" I didn't even go out with girls, let alone really know any, but somebody must have said something to some girls because the next thing I knew three girls asked me to go, but I politely said no. I didn't know how to dance, and I was always working if I wasn't studying. I still mowed lawns, played baseball, and did boy scouts.

After high school, I started looking for a car. Mom and Dad had a thing about cars. They wouldn't let one another drive their cars. You had to buy your own. My first car was a 1947 Fleetline Chevy. Soon after high school, I got a job at Nat Gas in Exton, which was down the road from us.

I learned how to fill propane tanks and helped deliver to homes, and after a while, I began installing stoves, water heaters, gas refrigerators, and space heaters.

The summer of 1949, after I got my car, we formed a baseball league. There was Exton, Frazer, Malvern, Lionville, Downingtown, West Chester, Marshallton, and Berwyn.

We had a good team. I used to play shortstop or left field. Sherman Trego was a pitcher. Ben pitched. Then there was Winnie Trego, Shorty Trego, Eddie Zonette, Carmen Zonette, Dick Schwanenberg, Bill Bray, Bob Trego, my brother Clyde, Bob Parry, Buddy Parry, Pete Moses, Jimmy Moses, Dick and Jack Green, George Krapf, Harry Delato, and a few I don't remember.

I was a little put out that I didn't get the chance to try out with the Phillies, but years later, seeing how they travelled coast to coast to play, I don't think I would have liked that too much. In years to follow, I put a lot of miles over the road.

At Nat Gas, Charlie Foy and I worked in the plant filling and painting tanks, and filling the tank trucks that delivered to homes. Also, we would get boxcars in with stoves that we would unload into the warehouse. We would see how fast we could unload a car—sometimes in about two hours or less. We had two 60,000-gallon propane tanks upgraded from a smaller tank, and we would unload the cars into the bigger tanks. Our transport would fill the lower tank, which I believe was about 30,000 gallons. Sometimes, we would switch tanks when we were filling small tanks. We had valves to turn on or off from the big tanks to the smaller tank. But every now and then, somebody would forget to turn off the upper tanks, and they would drain down to the small tank and blow the relay valve on the bottom tank. There was a can on top, and it would blow up in the air, and you'd run for cover. It would go straight up and back down.

---

Harold Witmer and I worked together a lot, for we used to haul what was called 420 tanks, which when full weighed 1,000 pounds. Wit and I would load them on a high truck, just the two of us. We got the name, "the bulls." We both weighed 140 pounds apiece and could lift 1,000 pounds.

Later, years after I left Nat Gas, I saw Ham and a couple fellows and they had a crane on the back of the trucks to lift those tanks. Ham said to the other two fellows, "Here's one of the guys we talk about." "We aren't strong or crazy like you two were," said the guys.

---

Pete Moses lived on the hill behind us, and he came to work with us. After I learned, and was out installing stoves for a while, Pete worked with me on the trucks until he learned. Then he was off on his own with a helper. We had our moments, some excitement now and then. I remember when I first started 40-hour weeks, I took home $31.69 for the week.

I guess in the fall of 1949 I bought my first new car, a 1949 Chevy from Sheeler's in Downingtown. It was black, and I would wash it every other day. Now we used to fill and paint tanks, mind you, and it was silver paint. Spraying tanks on the platform the spray travelled and low and behold, some of the spray made it onto my black car. I had to get it cleaned, and after that we used a paint room, so we didn't "paint" anymore cars.

Peg and Bud Epp lived in the house next door, so they watched out for the place. They had a black cocker spaniel, and she ran the place. She would bark at and chase anyone who didn't belong. I would be at Bud and Peg's at night. Bud and I would eat a whole half gallon of ice cream apiece before the night was over. They had two small boys, George and Gary, and guess what? Gary grew up and is now in Hollywood as an actor. He was a second to the Hulk, and he has other roles now. I haven't seen him for many years—he probably doesn't remember me. But I'm glad for him. I was hoping someday to see him once again.

I was still playing baseball and somehow I started seeing a beautiful young lady. She was going with a player from another team, but we hit it off. She worked for Bell Telephone in Paoli, then got transferred to West Chester, but didn't have any way to get there. So I said, "I have a car; I can take you." I would take her to work and when I got done I would go pick her up and take her home. After a few days we would stop and talk for a while and hug and kiss, but that was all. In our day, we were gentlemen and didn't do like they do today. It is a shame how things and people have gotten. We didn't have a lot but they were better times and we were better for it. What happened? The world is going to hell in a hand basket!

# THE 1950s

*I* had the scout patrol in Lionville from 1949-1951, and at that time they were building the Pennsylvania Turnpike. Me and some of the fellows in Lionville, we raced up on the dirt at night. The workers caught on to us running up there, and they had barricaded the bridges, and the road dropped off and down a slope. They took the barricade down, and one night, four of us were side by side and we went down this steep bank. How we didn't roll over, I don't know, but we didn't go back there again! They had closed off Route 100 going around Cackel's Garage. We were in the garage, and Mel Conner said he had gone around the curve at 50 miles per hour. I said, "If you could do it, so can I." I had my '47 Chevy at the time, and was going around the turn right on 50 miles an hour. I hit a sign on the road, and both doors flew open, but I held on and came back to the garage. Mel asked how fast I was going, and I told him 50 miles an hour, and he said, "You were the first."

We used to race up Milford Road at night. One night, George Ruark and I were in the front and Merreth Ruark was in the back, and there was a one-lane bridge and it had a bump on it. I was doing about 60 when I went over the bridge, and Merreth hit the roof and down he went. In a minute or two he got back up. Years later I saw him and asked how his head was, and he said, "It still hurts once in a while!" and we laughed. Later on in 1950, while working at Nat Gas, I had to haul a load of full tanks to our office in Philadelphia. I was to meet their driver, and he was to help me load a combination gas and coal stove, which weighed 1,200 pounds. He didn't show up, so I tried to load it by myself. As I started up on the tailgate, I slipped and the stove came down on me, hurting my back. Somebody in the alley heard me yell, and some guys came and got it off of me. I drove back to Exton, then had to go to the doctor. I was out for about ten days, and when I went back I couldn't do much lifting, so, that said, they didn't have much for me to do so they let me go. I got by for two or three weeks, and that was it!

I was off about three weeks and I was in a store one day and ran into Bill Murray, who owned Murray's Appliance in Paoli. We got to talking, for he was a friend of the family. In fact, my mom taught him in school years before. He told me to come down to the store and that he'd have a job for me.

I got back in shape and down to work at Murray's. It was light work at first, then I worked my way back into heavy lifting. We would carry stoves and refrigerators up two and three floors. I worked with electronics, installed air conditioners, and got into antenna work from and to oil burners, then worked back into delivering propane gas. We only handled 100-pound tanks there. I got so I was Bill's right-hand man.

I was making $1.50 per hour and I was working 100 hours a week. Back then, there was no time-and-a-half—it was all straight time. I later did everything, including doing the gas route and hauling appliances out of Philadelphia. I worked and got my strength back so he had me pulling loads of refrigerators, washers, dryers, and ranges out of the decks. I got to know my way around the city and I was back in shape. Back then there weren't many forklifts, so I used to double deck things by hand the old fashioned way—muscle.

One day on the dock this boy kicked a fellow in the head and knocked him down. They said he was a black belt. I saw this and I said to the fellow, "Tell him to do that to me." Her he comes—throws his foot up at me and I grabbed him by his leg and up and over my head and down on the concrete floor he went. And that's where he laid, and I said, "Don't mess with a farm boy." That ended the screwing around. Then a couple weeks later I come up on the platform and seven guys had a Jones Motor driver up against the wall and I said, "Looks like you have a problem." He said, "Yes, they want to kick the crap out of me," and I said, "That's not going to happen." One guy pointed at a big guy and said, "He's bad." Then I said, "Here is bad," and I got the biggest one and lifted him up over my body and threw him head first onto the floor. The others fled. A few weeks later, the big guy was on the dock and he saw me and came over with his hand up and said, "I don't want any trouble. Do you know how heavy I am?" He weighed 370 pounds and I tossed him like a feather. If you ever need help, call me.

I had to go pick up a water tower for an a.c. unit on 22$^{nd}$ Street and I was loaded except for a hole on the top deck. It was right at noontime and everybody was at lunch except a salesman. The tower weighed 400 pounds and the salesman said I had to wait until they came back from lunch and I said I'd get it. He said, "No way, that weighs 400 pounds!" I played him, for he didn't know me. I had a $50 bill in my pocket. I laid it on the table. He said he'd take that bet, so he put $50 on the table. I picked up the tower, put it up in the hole I had for it, turned and picked up the money, thanked him and said see you. Two weeks later I had to pick up another tower and the salesman was along with the other guys. He came over and said, "Bob, give me a chance to get my money back." So I let him talk two other guys into betting him, then I picked it up and put it in the hole I had for it. So he got his money back and said thanks.

I was working with Tim Geary who was the plumber on the housing project for Al Mandes. I guess we were there for about two months, then we had a job at the laundromat in Bryn Mawr. We had to install a 1,000-gallon water tank for hot water. A few years later I guess it started leaking and needed to be replaced. I was in Philadelphia and Bill called me and told me to stop at the laundromat on the way out and see what the guys needed help with.

I stopped and went in and one fellow asked how I got the tank in there. I pointed to a wall and said that wall wasn't there; so they had to cut the tank in two to get it out. Then they had to cut the new tank in half and weld it back together after they set it up in place.

One time I'll never forget, I had gone to Philadelphia and brought out a load of refrigerators—only a single deck for I wasn't feeling well that day. Bill said on an open truck the sky's the limit. A couple of days later I had refrigerators on the deck, washers on the second deck, and dryers on the third deck. I took a few wires down coming out Route 30 to Paoli.

Bill was on the back platform when I backed up. He said, "I heard you were coming. I got calls. Two decks from now on. I don't need anymore calls."

In 1950 Bill was in the Second World War, then went into the reserves. The draft was taking 18-20 year olds for the army and Bill came to me and said, "Bob I need you here for I don't have anybody that works like you. I will get you in the Air Reserve at Willow Grove air Base," which he did. I had a hip problem and they took me in anyway. I was there a year on the weekends then I was called up. I was on the drill field to march and I went down and the next thing I woke up in the Navy Hospital in Philadelphia. The doctor and commander stood there and he said, "Sailor, you are in big trouble. We found you have a bad hip." "Yes," I said, "I put it on the form when I signed up." They checked and came back and said I was right, so they released me with an honorable discharge.

    I was valuable to Bill because I could pretty much do everything, which was a lot. I still worked 100 hours a week. That's why he liked me, for nobody else would work like me. I went over to delivering propane, which we used 100-pound tanks which we had to change. I worked with Erne Wynn for about a year. Then I got another helper, Wilbur Hewitt, and we worked for about a year, then Wilbur left and became a cop in Malvern. Bill came to me and asked about another helper, and I said "I'll save you money. I'll run the route by myself," and he said okay. We still had two routes. Henry Drumhiller was the other driver and he didn't like doing it by himself. We had to take turns taking "out-of-

*Bob Reese, Navy, 1950*

gas" calls at night and weekends. Bill put a radio in my truck because when we were out we would call in twice a day to see if there were any calls. We would call collect and if they didn't have calls they would refuse the call.

I didn't like the radio so I didn't turn it on and Bill used to like to call a lot so he said, "I tried to get you," and I said, "I guess the radio doesn't work very well." He finally took it out and gave it to somebody else.

Franny Murray was Bill's brother and he took care of the warehouse, which was located in back of Franny's house. Franny also had school buses and he kept asking me to drive them. I told him he didn't have enough money for me to drive buses. No way would I drive a school bus.

It used to crack me up for every morning when the guys left the shop you would see at least ten trucks setting at Twaddler's Diner at the other end of Paoli.

It got so Bill would come looking for me because I told him I always stopped there for breakfast so he knew where to find me first thing in the morning.

The guys would see him coming and run out the back door and the cook and the man who worked behind the counter said, "You don't run," and I said, "no, because he is looking for me." The cook and I used to carry on. We would act like we were fighting and customers sitting next to me would move and we would laugh at them.

One afternoon there was a fellow who had ordered steak and three side dishes plus coffee. The cook and I started our routine and the guy picked up his dishes two at a time and moved to the booth. After that we said something to him and he said he thought there was going to be a fight and he was getting out of the way. Then we laughed and told him we did that all the time.

Bill said one day he needed me to help the fellows put a 10- ton a.c. unit in the diner. It was heavy and big. We moved it into the wall. We had to tip it over on end and walk it into the opening. Charlie Wright was behind the unit and had it ready to go in place when the guys slipped and let go of the unit and Charlie got pinned in behind and somehow being the bull I was, I literally climbed the wall and grabbed the top of the unit and pulled it out of the wall, saving Charlie from being killed.

---

I forgot about 1952. Dover Air Force Base was laying new runway for the C4s and they were using stone out of Bradford Hill's Quarry. There were 600 10-wheelers running from Downingtown, PA, to Dover, DE. The government told the state police to give these trucks the right of way so they could get the runways built. You talk about cowboys! We had them! They would run in packs of 20 trucks all overloaded for the trip. State troopers had set up road blocks. Bad idea when you got 20 ten-wheelers coming at you. What do you think happened to the road blocks? They were turned into splinters. I sometimes drove for Jack when he needed a break and we were in Smyrna early one morning and we always joked around with one another. Chuck came as I was getting ready to go and he hit me and over a table I went. I got up and everybody thought there was a fight coming and I said we do this all the time. He had a roll of dimes in his hand. It hurt. The next morning I got him coming in the door. I picked him up and threw him out the door.

---

Bill got me a new truck—a Dodge pickup. One day I was coming up to a red light. Luckily nobody was in front of me because when I hit the brake I couldn't stop, so I blew the horn and went through the light.

I called back to the shop and told them what happened and they sent another truck and we off-loaded the tanks. Then they towed the truck to the dealer's shop. The foreman got in it and drove it back and forth across the shop and it didn't do it again, so they said it must have been something I did. I got the truck back and a couple of days later it did it again so back to the shop it went again. The foreman again ran it back and forth. This time on the second time he was driving back and forth he went right through the wall and I said, "Now do you believe me?" and all I got was a look. Then we got a new truck which worked fine.

Back on the gas route I started getting more "out of gas" calls and they were on Henry's route and Bill asked what's going on. We checked tanks every month and if they used 45 pounds I would change the tanks. But Henry would let them go. Then they would run out. I sometimes would be out all night running calls being I was working all the time now. Sometimes, I would have 110 to 120 hours for the week which upset me, and Bill too. I told him, "Why don't I run both routes and I'll stop these out of gas calls," and he said ok. I would start about 6:00 a.m. and go until 6:00 p.m. In the meantime, Bill would be off to Willow Grove for two weeks and his wife entered the picture, which was not good. Soon after she was there her and I had it out. She didn't like me working all the hours and she was going to put a stop to it. Unbeknownst to her, Bill hired me and he was the only one that I answered to and not her, but she soon found out. I was a guy that went out of my way on the road to help people but I was one not to piss off.

I was strong. I could pick up 500 pounds back then so you see I wasn't one to cross, trust me. I had put some guys in the hospital a few times. Anyway, Mrs. Murray went behind Bill's back and hired another man. I had a habit of going off without hitting the time clock and I would write the time in. So one day this clown took my time card out and Hutch, who was like a dispatcher, said, "I wouldn't do that if I were you." He said, "Tell him I want to see him. If he wants to get paid he will start hitting the time clock." Hutch said, "That won't be good, trust me." And he was right. I came in to find my time card missing. I looked at Hutch. His expression told me what I needed to know. I went to the new employee's office and asked where my time card was and he said, "You are Bob." I said, "I am Bob Reese," then he said, "We need to talk," and I said, "really," and I grabbed hold of him and pulled him across his desk and knocked him back across it and he laid on the floor. Peg Murray came in and I walked right past her and went back to work.

Bill had given me a number if I had any trouble. I guess he knew there would be. I called him and he took time off and came back to see what happened. He read the riot act to his wife—"Nobody messes with Bob, you understand"—and went back to Willow Grove. I had no more trouble from these two again.

I always had busy days running gas routes on the truck to Philadelphia to pick up loads. We also had a big steel body truck to haul propane tanks for we had to haul empties to get filled and it was my job, too. Sometimes I would work around the clock. I had the routes caught up one time and Bill sent me to West Virginia to pick up a walk-in freezer for a diner we were working on. I was going all night and got back in at about 2:00 o'clock, and he sent me to Philadelphia to pick up a load of refrigerators. I got all the serial numbers but one—the refrigerator was up in the front of the load and Nick, who was in charge of everything, came in and got in my face about the serial number. So now he wanted me to unload the truck and find the serial number. I just got done driving all those hours and I was tired and was in no mood to be pushed around, which he found out the hard way. He got in my face and I hit him under the chin and drove him over a TV set. He hit the wall and he was out.

Bill was in the store and came out and I was still mad and tired and Bill asked what was going on. He saw Nick laying there and he turned toward me. Bill always wore a tie and it would be loose. I grabbed him by the tie and hit him too and down he went and then I left.

The next morning it was a little after 8:00 when I went in. Bill was coming down the stairs and said he needed to talk to me, and I said, "I guess I am fired," and he said, "No way. Just don't ever hit me like that again." I said okay and he handed me some work orders to do.

Before all of this went on, I got involved with a girl and got married. It was a disaster. The marriage only lasted a year. We had a son and I worked all the time. One day a buddy of mine came to me and put up his hands and said, "Don't hit me but I have something you need to know. Your wife is cheating on you," and told me where I could find her.

Later that day I stopped home and confronted her. She ran out and got in the car and I ran out to stop her. She ran right at me and I tripped and fell and she literally ran over me and she looked back. She saw me roll over to get up and she took off and never came back. Needless to say, I filed for a divorce.

I was on the stand and her lawyer asked me something that made me mad so over the railing I went and grabbed the lawyer by the throat. The judge said, "son, you need to come back and sit down." Then he called a recess and we went in his chambers. Judge Harvey was the judge. We went in his chambers and he told me I needed to settle down and take it easy. I asked if I could call my mom and he gave me the phone and I called my mom and told her what I did and she told me to put the judge on. I don't know what she said but all he was saying was, "yes Mrs. Reese, yes, yes, yes" and on and on. Then he hung up and said we would go out and take care of things. He took me off the stand as soon as we got out there. He went over a couple things and gave me a divorce. I went home and asked Mom what she said to the judge and she told me not to worry that she handled it.

Back to work I went. My gas route had 1,800 customers and I traveled to five counties. Everything was the same thing day in and day out up until 1954 when we started the Fire Company in Exton. It was called West Whiteland Fire Company. We bought a 1936 Dodge from Willow Street in Lancaster for $1,200.00. I was the first driver for the company. Barn fires were our biggest problem until Hurricane Hazel hit in 1954. I worked on the fire truck helping people. We had no power and trees and wires were down everywhere.

*West Whiteland Fire Company, 1956*

After working on the fire truck for several hours, I got a little nap and went to work at Murray's. All the power was out all around except Murray's Store. So off we went to customers with freezers loaded on our trucks and took them back to the store and plugged them in. Again I was the bull of the crew and Bill was on the end of a 22-foot full freezer. As we got to the door I had all the weight. Up the steps out of the cellar and onto the truck. He said, "I knew you could handle it," and I said, "Thanks a lot." Glad I was only 23 at the time and could handle a lot of weight. I still could lift 500 pounds over my head and I don't know why people ran from me. I am such a nice guy. Ha! It was several days before we got the power back on.

When I would get done with my gas route, then I would help out repairing and putting up antennas. I remember one time I had to go and meet a crew and help them with an antenna and rotor. It was a farmhouse near Glenmoore. I looked

*West Whiteland Fire Company, 1957*

at the chimney and told John Clarke that the rotor would take the chimney down if we put it on. But it was his job so he said that's where it was going to be put. I said, "Ok, but it's on you when it comes down and it did.

We did some crazy things in our day. We had a big job in Coatesville on Rt. 30. It was a two-story apartment building with 6-units, and there were four of us doing the job. We got to clowning around on the roof and acting like we were shooting at one another and across the street was a bus stop. Jack had a pole in his hand and acted like he was shooting at me and I was running across the ridge of the roof. I dropped down like I was shot and I fell down and was rolling down the roof and grabbed onto the ridge and then we heard screaming across the street at the bus stop. Here, a little old lady saw us and passed out. Our trucks were sitting out front and somebody got the phone number and called the store and we got the devil when we got back.

One time Ray and I were out back of West Grove on a farm on a big old three-story house with a big chimney with three flues coming out of it. Bricks were loose and I had Ray hanging over the chimney and the bricks started falling out and I grabbed him before he fell. It was a long way down.

I was in Coatesville on a double home and I got good reception on one side. But on the other house I couldn't get good reception. So I got the two together and told them what I could do. Back then it was flat 300 on wire. So I told them I could add 10 feet to the one with good reception and both would have reception. Then they could split the cost instead of two antennas, and they agreed.

Getting back to the propane, I got a call to get to Oxford as quick as I could. There was an explosion and fire. When I got there, the fire trucks were there and the chief came over and said it must of come from the basement. A man was home. He was in the bathtub when the gas exploded. He had just moved in and we discovered the previous owners had put a potato on the end of the tubing, which when the new fellow turned the gas on the potato went flying and left the gas filling the basement and caused the explosion. The man was in the bathtub when the firemen arrived. What an embarrassment!

Back at the store, Bill was away at Willow Grove for his two weeks and his wife started her crap again. She and I had it out and I quit. Bill found out about it and kept calling me to come back. I said, "Bill you have to live with it. I don't."

I went to work for Clayton R. Erner Milk Trucks hauling cans from the farmers. I had 23 stops. The first stop I picked up at 2:00 a.m. on Route 282 at Lindell then on to Glenmoore for two more stops. Then back 82 to 322 for one stop at the corner of 82 and 322. Then onto south of Honeybrook, where I had two stops just before Honeybrook and had to turn right before Honeybrook and picked up two stops. The irony is I had eight stops and they were all Ben Stoltzfus. You had to go by the middle name. Then up to Morgantown and across Route 23 to the next stop back off of 23, then back to 23 to Knauertown for a stop on 23, then to Pughtown and one more stop off Pughtown Road. Then it was on to Lansdale to Martin Centers Dairy.

Usually, the truck ahead would be loading empties when I got there. You unloaded onto a chain belt, which took the cans in to the milk room. I had 300 cans and 10 to 12 minutes to unload. By the time you got the last can off the empties were coming out.

I worked there until December when I came down with pneumonia and was in bed for a couple of weeks. I was home in bed and the wife was at work when the fire monitor went off—"Lady in the house and house is on fire." What did I do? I jumped out of bed and drove the truck to the fire, got lady out of house and I was done. They had to take me home and I got hell from the doctor and wife. There aren't many men willing to run into a burning building and someone had to do it—it might as well have been me. I guess I am one of the crazy ones. God's always with me and I thank him for that, for you know without God we are nothing. With him you can do a lot.

Now on another note, I got ahead of myself. That happened in 1955, but in 1954 I was back at Murray's on the back platform one afternoon. A girl that worked at Bell Telephone right behind me was walking home and I had watched many days and would say hi, so this day I asked to talk to her and she said yes. I jumped down from the platform and went up to her and said, "I am Bob Reese. As you know I work here," and she said, "I have seen you often. My name is Celestine Price and I live on the north side of the railroad on Central Avenue." So I said, "I live in Exton on Route 100 with my dad and mom. I work a lot so I don't get to go anywhere to see girls. I would like to come see you sometime if you would like that" and she said, "Sure, just tell me when." So we went to the movies on Saturday night and hit it off and the next weekend I was invited to Sunday dinner and met her mom and dad and we hit it off right away. We were together for about a year and then we got married on October 22, 1955. I was still driving milk trucks. We lived in an apartment in Paoli for about a year and in the meantime Dad and Mom said they were going to build us a house in the back field. I believe we finished up pretty well in 1956 when we moved in. Backing up, when we started building the house they told us we might as well move in with them so we would be close.

Dad and I built the house and Clyde would come and help out when he could. We built a house with two bedrooms, one bath, kitchen, dining room and living room, a cellar, an attic, a breezeway, and a two-car garage, on one and a half acres. Dad and Mom gave us the land along with the house. They did that to keep me close. In the meantime we went and got a dog. Sally liked cocker spaniels, so we found a black cocker and brought it home to Mom and Dad. I had left my job hauling milk and went to work at the roller rink that the fire company built in Exton. That way, we could work a day on the house.

There was a train wreck at Ship Road that kept us busy for a while. I drove and I also worked with the fire police, where I directed traffic that night and that's when I first met Kip. He was a railroad police officer and we hit it off right away. And how that happened, I was directing traffic at Ship and Kint Road. We had Ship blocked and some guy wanted to go down to see what happened and was told he couldn't go down. I was standing in front of his car and he came at me and I went up over his head. Kip saw that and stopped him and pulled him out of the car and turned and asked if I was okay. It took a couple of days to clean that up. Then there were a few barn fires, mostly in the Lionville area, and they would keep us busy for days.

In the meantime, one day we were working on the house putting on the roof and Candy, that was our cocker, came by and I saw her walking around. She did this many times, so I didn't think anything of it. We kept working, putting shingles on the roof. Next thing I heard was a rattling on the ladder. Still, I wasn't paying attention. Then I looked up and there

Candy was looking at me. She climbed up the ladder all the way to the roof. I had to get her off the roof. I got on the ladder and Dad handed her to me to take back down, and told her to go down to Mom. She was out watching and Candy went back down to Mom.

After we got the roof finished, the electrician got the wiring finished, we put up the drywall, and after that the contrac-

*Our wedding day*

tor would put the metal corners on. But I did it and when Mr. Ford came to give me a price he checked the metal corners and said I made them stick out too far. He said they do ¾" and I had them a whole 1". I said, "That's what I want. So charge me extra, but that's what I want." After that we put down oak flooring and Dad sanded the floor and got it ready and asked what we wanted to do with it. I said I would get down and hand rub the floor with linseed oil. That brought out the grain in the oak and then we varnished over that. It turned out to be one beautiful floor and it was worth it.

I believe that it was in 1956 that the old feed mill in Exton caught fire and burned down. I was there and we dug out under the main floor stuff from back in the Second World War used for putting out fire from bombs if we were ever attacked, which never happened, thank God. I got under the floor working a hose on the fire when the floor gave way, falling down on top of me. Guys who were right there wondered how they were going to get me out and I said calmly, "Get those two blocks and be ready. Put them under the floor when I raise it up." One said no way, but with "God's" help I lifted the floor enough for them to put blocks under and I told them to pull as I wrapped the hose around one. That turned out to be an all-nighter. The fire was east of Nat Gas, so we put a truck up there to put out anything flying that way for sparks were driven by the wind.

Sometime in 1956, Earl talked me into going to work for Beloit Eastern in Downingtown. They made paper machinery. I learned how to run a big planer and didn't take long to get good at it. It wasn't too long after, I was there maybe six to eight months, that we went on a 12-hour shift and in a week or so we started seven days a week. The only way you got a day off was if the other fellow work 36 hours before he got to go home and

*Sally and Candy, 1959*

*Bob and Candy*

if he wanted off, then I had to work 36 hours. I guess about a year went by, and they had a family member come in from Beloit as a time study. He and a foreman from the shop would go around to the different machines and they would change feed and speed of the machines and when they took pieces off the machine they would walk away. I watched them do this to a number of guys so I said to my buddy next to me, "They won't do that here," and walked away. The irony of things was that my brother Earl became head boss of the machine shops, so this was going to be interesting because I was my own man and didn't take much crap off anybody including my brother. He used to go tell Mom about me sometimes but he didn't know that didn't do any good. So here they came down to my machine and I shut my machine down and said to the two of them that I had a program. I told them to go get their coveralls and put the piece back on the planer or else they would be headed for the hospital and they laughed. Bad idea! They started to walk away. I waited until they got to the end of my planer, which was 40 feet, then I grabbed both by their belts and literally dragged them back to the machine. "Now, what's it going to be? Put it back on or off to the hospital, and if you really make me mad, it could be the morgue."

They went and got their coveralls and put the parts back on the machine and left. Next, a runner came over and said, "Hey, Bob, your brother Earl wants you in his office."

I went in to see Earl. "You want to see me?" "Yes." "What's this I hear you just did out there?" "You have a pair of jerks running around out there speeding up machines and knocking stuff off the machines and walking away. They weren't going to do that to me. So we have a problem. Fire me if you have to save face and don't bother running to Mom. She knows how I am, and you know I don't take crap from nobody, even you." Then he said, "Go back to work and don't kill anybody today."

Earl Slern was my foreman and he came around after that and said he was glad somebody stood up to them. I was getting tired of them knocking pieces off the machines and walking away.

I was good at running the planer—so good they had me rework the inspection tables. I had a bet with the foreman I had the run-in with for $100.00. He used to run the same planer years ago. I told him I would have the table without a one inch of the whole length of the table and I did. He paid but he wasn't happy.

One day around noontime I responded to a fire call. I was home and heard there was a lady in a house, trapped by fire. When I got there I was the first truck in. I put the pumps in gear, told another to watch, and I went through the front door and found there was no floor. I dropped down into the basement and on top of the fire. Luckily, George Ruark from Lionville Fire Company was right behind me and heard me yell. They dropped a 1 ½ hose down and I tied it around me and they pulled me out. It got a little hot before I got out. Afterward we found a lady laying on a day bed dead. Earl Stern was Chief of Alert Fire Company and they were there to help. He said whoever was the first truck in, would have to stay until the coroner got there and took the body away. Being my foreman, he said he would take care of my time card. Beloit was good about paying the fireman when they missed their shifts fighting fires.

Downingtown called us in to help fight a hot fire at Griffith's Hardware Store which lasted a couple of days. I was up on the roof next door and I went to step around a corner of the building and damn near slipped into the fire. But Penny was right behind me and grabbed me and saved me from falling.

In in the spring of 1955, Farrells had a farm on Route 100, north of Eagle on the left. It is a housing development now. Back then they had a pig farm and the barn caught fire. We went to help Lionville and little pigs were running around on fire. We saved a lot but had to kill some and I woke up every night for a long time with nightmares. I never drank until that night. When we got back we went to the Exton Lodge and

*Bob the fireman*

I had my first drink and had a few that night. There are two things you never get over as a fireman fighting fires: burning animals and humans. When you find a person, that smell never leaves you, trust me. I have seen a few.

    1957 got pretty wild for the fire companies for it was a dry year. We had a lot of field fires back then. I remember one afternoon a field caught fire right off Route 100, a field on the left. I went in with the dodge and Bill had the LaFrance. I was first in getting the fire out but the exhaust from the LaFrance was setting more fires, so I called to him that he was setting more fires and to stop. Next thing, there was even a fire on the railroad, which took some time to put out.

    I am not sure what year it was, but we had a forest fire west of Clifford Nursing Home, and those years we didn't have a lot of help in the fire company.

    It was in the woods west of the nursing home and we had to call Linoville, Downingtown, East Whiteland and before it was contained we had 13 companies plus the Willow Grove canteen buses. We had tried to contain the fire but the wind changed and blew the fire east through the home. That's when we called for all that we could get. We had to evacuate the home, which was a project in itself. We were all glad we didn't lose any lives.

    In September it was dry and I guess there were bad brakes on a train car. It was setting fires from Downingtown to Berwyn which turned into a disaster. It took about 15 to 20 companies to get it under control. Paoli and East Whiteland had engines caught in the fires in the field. Smoke took the oxygen out of the air and the trucks stalled out and burned up. Guys had to run to safety. I heard somebody from Berwyn call for police to shoot the snakes that came off the railroad car out of the west.

Then we had a couple of barn fires to round out the year. The barn fires we had were far from water, so we had to lay a lot of hose. It was nothing for us to lay a couple miles of hose at a barn fire.

Still at Beloit, we were running seven days a week and twelve hours a day. That kept up until March of 1958, which became a bad time for us. Beloit laid off 3,000 people on the 18th of March, and I was one of them, and it had started to snow. It was a wet, heavy snow and kept on snowing all the way through the 21st of March. I helped out at Jack Funderwhite's Esso Station on the corner of Routes 30 and 100. I helped Jack put chains on cars and we got soaking wet but kept on going all night. In the morning I told Jack I had to get home, which was across the road. I had to check on Mom and Sally. By then we had 18-20" of snow. I called Channel 6 and told them we had 20" of snow and they didn't believe me for they had hardly any at that time. On the 21st I measured 52" on Route 100 at the crossroads. It was wet and heavy. We lost power for ten days.

Parry's had a big dairy farm and couldn't find a generator anywhere and they were milking 300 cows. They milked around the clock. That's a hell of a lot of cows to milk by hand. Morris Seeds sold snowmobiles. He had three, so he let us use them to go fight fires for nobody could get the trucks out. We would strap Indian tanks and fire equipment on them and go to the fires. Also, we used them to bring pregnant women into the firehouse and helicopters from Willow Air Station would fly them to the hospital. They could only use bulldozers to plow the snow, for it was heavy and deep for the other plows. They had a tanker type helicopter to go to the farms to haul the milk to the dairies.

We had a fireplace so we were able to keep warm, and being an old boy scout, I could cook in the fireplace. Fortunately, it wasn't real cold out and we melted snow for water. Anything that needed to be cold, we put out in the snow. It took until the end of May to get rid of the snow. I was out of work for about a month. Then I found a job with a land clearing outfit, Seller Brothers out of Sellersville, PA. Charley and Chuck owned and operated the business. First job I was on was widening Route 202 south of West Chester to Painter's Crossroads. I helped cut up trees and I had a gas can running down the side of the road burning off the honeysuckle and high weeds. I started out small and built up the fire and it caught up with me once. I had the honeysuckle burning, then I would go a little ways and spread gas and the fire would light it up. Once, I dropped the gas too close and I heard a bang and I found out how fast I could jump the guardrail to get away from the flames. I was really careful after that. We cleared all the way to Painter's Crossroads, then we were finiahed that job.

We then moved on to Route 1 by around Media. After clearing the trees we piled them up in a huge pile. We had a Second World War jeep with a Cadillac engine mounted on the back of the truck with a six-foot airplane propeller. When we put that up to the pile of trees, we used one truck and mixed gas and the propeller would blow air through the pile. After five minutes we would have a roaring fire.

One day we were down at the quarry clearing and there was an empty dynamite shack so we pushed trees around it and were going to burn it along with the trees. We left at 4:00 that day, for we were planning to start early to burn before daylight. We got there at 5:00 a.m. and lit the pile and about that time here comes fire trucks and one of Glasgow's pickups blowing their horns. The pickup came up and the guy said there was actually dynamite in the shack. We yelled to get the heck out of there and stop those fire trucks. We would get the dozers and try to stop the fire. Another fellow and I grabbed fire suits and got the dozers into the pile and pushed it away from the shack, thank God, or we would have been toast. So goes the life of the land clearers.

So in the meantime, Seller Brothers was union and I had 90 days' grace until I had to join the union and Charlie knew I wasn't going to join. A couple of union strong arms came up in the woods one day and one of the fellows said, "Here comes trouble." I said, "What do you mean?" He said, "The union guys are looking for you." I told the dozer operator to dig a hole and I would take care of them. He said, "No you can't do that!" I said, "Why not? We shot horses when they went lame." I didn't kill them, I just roughed them up a little. See, I think people don't always realize that you don't mess with farm boys, trust me. Charlie had to let me go because I was not going to join the union, period!

## The 1960s

*B*ack in the day, men didn't mess with me, at least those who knew me. I helped many people out of trouble in the day, in fact I saved a state cop once. Four guys had him pinned down on Route 30 at Ship Road with four shotguns. I came in off the road, slowed my truck down and jumped out hitting the ground rolling. I came up with a .38 in hand and said, "Drop your guns or die." I guess that "die" got them and they dropped their guns. Joe said, "Am I glad to see you" and thanked me. I said, "After we get them rounded up you might want to go home and change your pants," and he said, "you got that right."

  I've done a lot of crazy things in my day, but I was always looking out to help someone all the time. If I didn't help somebody in any given day, that day was a loss to me. I always found good in people, no matter rich or poor. I know back when we were building the house for Sally and me, people would come along and ask me to help with a job, a fundraiser or some sort of project. One day Sally asked, "Why do people always ask you to do things?" I said, "I don't know why." I asked a lady one day why everybody targeted me to do things and she said, "When you need something done you ask a busy person, which is you. Nobody around works like you do and they know this." And they were right. I was working all the time.

We did also take time out to go out and party and dance the night away. After Beloit, I helped Jack Funderwhite at the Esso station on the corner and I did jobs for people around their houses. Then I drove dump trucks for Paul Martin and after a while Paul and I got together and bought Twin City Beverage in Spring City. We put up $10,000 apiece to start and went from there. Soon after Paul and I took over the business, the union guys came in and told us we had to join the union even as owners and that didn't set too well with us. If we wanted to get beer we had to join, so we had to join even though we didn't like it. It took some time for Paul and I to get in with the people, so to speak. I'll never forget our first year there coming into Christmas season. We had 24 inches of snow and nobody could get in to us. Christmas Eve day they finally got us plowed out. The people came all day, and later that night one helper asked when we were going to close. I told him when they stop coming in, and that was about 4:30 a.m. and I still had deliveries on the way home. I got home about 7:00 a.m. and I was done. I went to bed, got up about 3:00 p.m. Then I went to Mom's for dinner.

The irony of the whole thing was, before the snow came, all the distributors said to load up and they would hold the checks until after Christmas. So while we couldn't get anywhere, we added up the check bill to find out how much we were overdrawn. It was over $40,000, and this was our first Christmas, so we didn't know what would happen but thank God we made enough in one day to make up for it. Then the following week was just about as good. Then, after New Year's, things died down for a couple of weeks. Christmas and New

*Twin City Beverage, 1963*

*Twin City Beverage, 1964*

Year's you have a lot of people, who you only see once a year, but we had our firehouses and taprooms to get us going, as well as the regular guys.

We joined groups to get ourselves known in the towns. Twin City Beverage is what we went by. We were in an alley in an old garage when we bought the business, but we soon found the old schoolhouse on Bridge Street for sale. We bought that and built an addition onto the back of the school and made a drive-thru operation. While we were renovating the place, Paul's brother, Bob Martin, was like me. Working with him, I put the roof on the drive-thru and in the meantime we had contracted with County Con to put in the driveways and parking lot.

Before all of this, we needed to buy a walk-in cooler for the beer. A salesman for Bally ------ and Cooler came and gave us a price, which was too high for us. I told him that I could build one for about $3,000.00-their price was about $7,000.00. I told him unless he came down a lot we couldn't do business with him. A few days went by and he came back and said it was their slow season so they came down to $3,000.00, but this was only delivered, not set up, which was okay with me. I had help to set it up so I told him how to load the truck so when we put it together it was the right way I needed to set it up. The salesman said he would stop and see how we were making out after he got out of church and I told him that would be okay but I didn't think we would be there because my mom had a duck dinner that would be ready at 12:00 and she did not want us to be late. We opened the trailer up at 8:00 a.m. and closed the two doors to the cooler at 11:00 a.m. and went home. On Monday morning, the salesman showed up and said he had never seen a box that big set up that quick. He wanted to know if he could hire me to work for them? I told him no thanks.

After this, Bob Martin and I put the roof on the drive-thru. While doing so, we had the first half of the roof on and were working on the back end over the cooler. The contractors were loading their equipment and they headed down one side of the building where the trucks were pulling up to load and leave. I said, "Wait a minute, you didn't finish the job." He said he hadn't had that in the bid, and I said, "I showed you what I wanted done and you gave me a price on that." Well, we had words, and I told him it had to be done. I was hot—so hot that I was pulling a rafter on the roof walking backwards and walked off the roof and fell on a pile of stones. A piece of stone went into the corner of my eye. Bob took me to the doctor's and luckily the stone didn't hit the eye. I came back and went on to finish the roof. We moved into the schoolhouse in the spring and people liked the drive-thru part. We had three trucks that we used for deliveries and had a one-ton truck to haul soda from other distributors. Paul would go over to the bar getting customers and I would take care of the store and go pick up beer and sodas.

A while into 1960 I came down with internal bleeding and was rushed to the hospital in West Chester, which is now Paoli Hospital. Dr. Kistler was my doctor. They had to give me blood and he said I would be there for a while. I told him the nurses wouldn't put up with me very long.

Old Doc Kistler and his son Phil came in together to tell me I was staying for a few days and said there would be no telephone, and no visitors except for my wife. I told them I was not going to stay more than three or four days; I was going home. I said, "Hey doctor, I'll go home and do what you tell me." They thought about that a while and said, "In three days we will let you go home. But if you turn for the worse, you will be back in and we expect nothing out of you. Agreed?"

Later, I found out they bet I would be back in the hospital in two weeks. But I fooled them. I went home and rested and did what they told me to do.

In two weeks I went to the office and Phil took me in his office to check me out and everything was good. Phil said, "One day Dad went in to see you and you must have told him something, because he came back to the office and walked in with a lit cigarette in both hands and I knew you did something. I had never seen him like that before."

I was back to work for a while then Paul and I had a disagreement about some things and it was mutually agreed that I would buy him out. Then, soon after buying Paul out we started having trouble with the union again. I was having trouble with Frank DaDelasio coming around trying to steal customers. So I went down to Phoenixville to his taprooms in the daytime—that's when owners generally worked. I'll never forget we had PRs back then. It was a Reading beer and I would sell it for $2.95 a case. I would say to the owner, who was the bartender, "Is Frank taking good care of you?" for everybody sold PRs. He asked why and he said he has a new price now, I believe it's $2.65 a case and he asked if I'd sell it to him for that price and I said no, but Frank could.

I went into about six bars that day, and in the afternoon when I got back to the shop he had called looking for me. Then about that time he called and I answered the phone. He was yelling and I left him yell for a minute. Then I told him to stay in Phoenixville and I would stay in Spring City, but he kept trying to get my bars.

One day Ray Gentle, the Budweiser salesman, came in and asked if I wanted to have fun with Frank, and I asked why. Ray said Frank's brother-in-law owned the bar on the corner across from Frank's place. He owed Frank money and Frank wouldn't give him any beer until he paid him. Ray said he would give me an order and pay me cash so I said okay. We could have put it on one truck but I wanted to really make Frank mad. We even turned around in his driveway. He came out yelling and shaking his fist.

He did steal an account of mine but that didn't last long for I caught him stealing and they threw him out and told all the bars in town. It pays to be honest.

In this period of time I believe we got into a fight with the union and they put up pickets around all the beer distributors in the county. We had pigeons on the roof, so I would go out and shoot up in the air and the union got upset with me. But I said I was shooting at the pigeons. We would watch the pickets and if they stopped, the cops would haul them off to jail. This also made all of us have to haul our own beer from the city.

I went into Scott & Grauer to pick up Ballantine, which was popular in those days, and the union guys thought they were going to rough me up until they saw a .38 on my side. It tends to change a guy's mind. Then the manager came out and told them to unload, and load me, and not to mess with my truck if they didn't want me to kick their butt, for he had seen me fight and knew they didn't want to go there. Spaz Beverage sent a truck there and while the driver was in the office they cut a couple of tires and he had to get them changed before he got home.

A union guy by the name of Grubb came in my place with two enforcers. It was a bad idea—you don't mess with a farm boy. He tried to get me to agree to their contract but I said no and his boys looked like they wanted a piece of me. So

*Bob and beer truck, 1965*

I grabbed one, picked him up and threw him out the door and then the other one ran. They left really fast and didn't come back. We went on to take the union to court and finally beat them in court. We got the union out of Chester County beer distribution. I have to laugh now in 2013, after all the franchise beers were bought out, Spaz Beverage being the last, all beer comes from Philadelphia and with union drivers. So after all of this we moved on and had no more trouble from the unions.

During this time back home in Exton, the wife and I would go out doing a little drinking and dancing. In fact, I wasn't too bad for an old farm boy. Early during the winter of 1960 we had a fire at the Eagle Tavern in Eagle, about four to five miles away from our station. We got on the road and it took us a half an hour to get there. Al Shanders, Ed Goldberg, and I went up on the back roof over the kitchen, which was all ice. As we were there, putting water on the fire, Al Shanders slipped, hit Ed Goldberg, then me, and down off the roof we came. I was on the bottom. I hit the ground on my back, then Ed hit on top of me, and Al landed on Ed. It knocked the wind out of them, but I was okay. We went back up on the roof, but we tied ourselves to a pole.

The beer business was pretty much routine. We had, back then, home delivery and also delivered to taprooms. On weekends we would visit family and go out with friends. Every Sunday we went to Sally's mom and dad's for dinner. They lived across the tracks from us. Saturday nights we would go to the Collegeville Inn for a buffet, for that was the place to go. After a while, they got so busy you had to wait a long time, so we went across the bridge to the Persimmon Bridge Hotel. They had the same food and no waiting time.

We started going there every Saturday night and got friendly with the owners. When they got busy and we went in, they said to go to the bar and they'd get us a table, for they had long lines by that time.

I believe in June each year the Phoenixville Lion had a clam bake and they bought their beer and soda from Twin City Beverage, which was me. Joe McConnell was in charge, and invited my wife and me as his guests. It turned out to be an all-night occasion. After we cleaned up at the clam bake, we went to the bar where we helped. We left there about 5:00 a.m., so we didn't get much sleep.

Herm Walters and Charlie Christy worked for me while we were in Spring City. Later the next year I built a building next to my house in Exton. I had Sherman Trego do the cement and blockwork, because we grew up together, went to school and played baseball together, and he became a good stonemason.

I gave Sherman $8,000.00 up front so he could get material for the job, and I said, "Sherman, when you get the block up for the first floor, you can have a day to do the other jobs. Then be back the next day, ready to finish your job."

Sherman finished up the first floor about 4:00. I had Jack Nauton put up the steel girders and that day, before 5:00, Davis Lumber delivered my lumber for the floor. I had Clyde, my brother, who was a contractor, come to help and I had Herb, another brother, and two workers help, and we worked half the night and put up 3" x 12" rafters for the floor. Then by early morning, I had a crew for my guys and we laid 6" x 2" tongue and groove flooring, with 60 penny nails. By 2:00 we were finished the floor, and by 2:30 they unloaded block for the top wall. The next morning Sherman and his crew laid block to the roof. The next day we put up the rafters and roofed it in with 1" marine plywood. Leo Curdo Roofing put the finishing touch to the roof with tar and paper.

Clyde, Herm, Herb, and myself took the walk-in apart in Spring City and put it back up at Exton. We had to fill 14" in front of the building so as to make the parking lot level with the building's floor. We filled just a few feet at a time against the front wall, to prevent it from caving in. From the day we dug the footers, it took us nine days to finish and move in and open up.

A while after we had been open, a trucker stopped in and asked me how long it took us to build the building. He said he went by every week and all at once there was a building that appeared to come up out of the ground. I told him from the day we poured the footers it took us nine days to finish and open the doors for business.

Backing up a bit, early in 1960, the wife and I were sitting at a red light on Route 30 and a young boy hit me in the rear end and I got hurt. My back hurt so the next day I got x-rays. You could take a knife and cut me on my left side and I couldn't feel anything. It took 13 months until they finally sent me to Philadelphia to get a scan where they found a pinched nerve. They used eight wide straps to hold me down, but when the dye hit my head I broke all eight straps. The guys grabbed me to finish the x-ray. They found the pinched nerve and got it out and I was alright. A couple weeks later I was back to work. While I was off, my brother Herb took a route I ran. There was a dog at the one place that would get up on a shed and when I got out and came around back of the truck he used to jump down on me and I would fall down. Then we would play for a while. I forgot to tell Herb about this and he was surprised and it scared him. Herb said, "What else am I going to have happen?" I said, "Nothing that I know of."

We still had home delivery and I had tap rooms, too. I'll never forget the Exton Lodge. They had a dining room and a big bar. I went in one day with a delivery and I saw the bartender setting up seven shots and seven beers at each stool and I asked what that was all about and he told me that the guys from Autocar only had 20 minutes for lunch and he said they came in and downed the seven shots and beers in 20 minutes and then went back to work.

I didn't open the doors until 10:00 a.m. or 11:00 a.m.—that way I could go pick up beer from other distributors. I had a beer license and we had to buy from I.D.'s or breweries. I bought beer off of Spaz Beverage, Lunai Beverage, Matt Lamb Beverage, Strafford Beverage, and Terrizzi Beverage.

Then Scott & Grauer delivered Ballantine beer. I would go to Reading Brewery in Reading for PRs and other beer. Yuengling Brewery delivered. Then I got Coke from Coatesville, Canada Dry out of Philadelphia, and Frank's Beverage out of Philadelphia. I would get whole loads of Frank's Soda at a time, and have them come early. I would give the driver money to go over to the Exton Diner for breakfast, and we would have it unloaded and the empties on the truck by the time he got back.

I guess it was late afternoon or early evening when the Downingtown Fire Company called us to help out at Gindy's Trailer, which turned out to be a big fire. They sent us in behind the building, and it was a good thing I had the windows down. Block was flying in the cabin as I was going along the side of the building to get to the back. I kicked my pump in gear and told another to watch, and I went into the building. Propane tanks were in the fire, and we got blown out of the building. I got off the block and said, "I need two to go back in with me, and they said, "No way are we going in there with you, you are crazy."

But we got back in the building, and saved a couple trailer loads of tires and some machinery, but it turned out to be a total loss. It was an all-nighter and into the next day.

In the spring and summer we had field fires and had a few barn fires. We could drive the cows out of the barn, but the horses were another story. We had to lead them out of the barn and fence them in or they would go back into the barn.

One call we had a truck on fire on Route 100, up past Marchwood Center. When we got there, Lionville called and said the truck had .38 ammo for the Ohio State Police on board. So I pulled up short of the truck and somebody said to get closer, but I said there was ammo in the truck and to get the water gun in place, for the bullets were going off and flying wildly out the sides of the trailer.

I forget what year it was but we had a barn fire at Whitford on Route 30. It was the old Wilson farm. Their barn was right off of Route 30. It had 200 tons of hay in it, so it was a long time before we could get it under control.

AT&T's television cable that went to the west coast got burned and was down, and the heads of AT&T were screaming at us to get the fire out so they could repair the cable. We had plenty of water because Valley Brook was only a quarter mile away and we were used to laying a lot of hose, for back then there were no hydrants to hook up to. It was well into the night that we could get in with water to knock the hay apart and get the fire knocked down.

Even after our busy schedule, we found time to go to the Pin Bowl Inn in Frazier, which was one of the bars I served. We worked hard in our day, but we also played hard.

I would be up early every morning doing something around the place. We opened up at 10:00 a.m. and were open until 9:00 p.m. I would stay until 5:00 or 6:00, and Phil Chamblin worked from 6:00 to 9:00 every night.

My brother, Herb, had a big pool that we helped him with. Sylvan Pool put in the pool and we poured the concrete for around the pool. In the summertime when I was busy and worked late, I would go over and take a dip in the pool, then go home for a nap. One day we were there, we heard a scratching noise, and looked at the corner of his house, and Candy was digging a hole there. Herb said, "What is she doing?" And I said, "You have a mouse there." She came away with a mouse, and they laughed. I said, "She is a good mouser." I had soda machines that I put out at construction jobs, and in later years I sold ice. Union jobs required ice on the job at 68 degrees. I was the only game in town that would deliver to the job. They built storage boxes so I could come early in the morning, to have ice on the job for when they started work. I took care of school jobs and building and road jobs as well.

In the early days, the machines were mostly bottle machines and I used Frank's Soda, which was big in the 60s, but has gone out of business since.

I used Coke, Pepsi, and Canada Dry. In fact, Canada Dry rented machines to me, and I bought some. Rubino landfill was a big stop back then. They were good for about 25 cases a week. It was owned by Sam and Ted Rubino, who became County Commissioners in later years. I was also in politics at one time. I was a Democratic committee man in the 60s.

Morris Seeds lived across the tracks from us. We were best friends, and we went out a lot. Saturday nights we might go to the American Legion in West Chester, or the Elk Club in West Chester.

At the Elk Club we would run into Jimmy John, who had Jimmy John's Hot Dog place on Route 202 south of West Chester. Jimmy John was a pretty good singer in his day, and we all gathered around and sang songs until 5:00 a.m., then went to the diner for breakfast, then home. Morris was a J.P. and had XL since service. I remember one Saturday night we were at the Legion until about 3:00 a.m. and when we got to Morris' house there was a state cop with a DUI and here we had to help Eve Seeds into the house. Good thing she wasn't trying to drive.

Sally, who is my wife, worked at Deluxe Check Printers in Paoli, PA, for years. They would have a Christmas banquet every year at the VFW in Paoli. We would have a cocktail hour and dinner. Then on to music and dancing the night away. I wasn't too bad of a dancer.

Our life kind of revolved around our cocker spaniel, Candy—so she was the love of our life. She loved to ride. She was all black, except for a white spot on her chest. She was something else. In bed she would work her way up on my pillow at night and lay right against my head, and I in my sleep would move and one night I fell on the floor and I turned the light on and she was looking down at me with a grin. Something else she was good at, was breaking wind and looking around like, "What, I didn't do that." But we loved her anyway. One time she was out in the field and a pheasant came out of the tall grass and they looked at one another and didn't know what to do. With the Seeds next door, they had a German Sheperd, and they got along pretty well.

---

### A BRIEF HISTORY...

Jim John, after six other ventures in the food business, started the open-air Pipin' Hot on the new Wilmington Pike in early May 1940. The first addition was made that fall to winterize. Summer of 1941 saw three more additions. It stayed that way through WWII and was managed by his wife, Louise John. Soon after returning from overseas, in 1945, the property was purchased from our neighbors, Elizabeth and William Heyburn. In 1948, a new building was erected and business continued to grow! However, 12 years later, it was demolished to make way for a four-lane highway. A new 100-foot building was erected just north of the original site in 1960. Inside seating was provided by an addition in the spring of 1973.

As of December 2005, Jimmy John's is now owned and operated by its longest-standing employee, Roger Steward, who began working at Jimmy John's in 1974. He considers it his privilege to continue what Jimmy John started so many years ago. We thank each and every one of you who continue to make Jimmy John's a favorite place to bring your family and enjoy the history of this local legend.

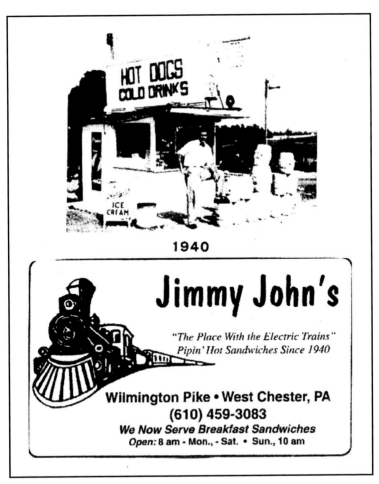

*Jimmy John's Ad*

On the weekends, we were up at the Seeds' until 4:00 or 5:00 in the morning. One time I got on Eve about something and she didn't say much, and that Saturday night we were there until 5:00 a.m. About 9:00 to 9:30 I was at Howard Johnson's there in Exton, and Morris came through the door and said, "Reese, you're welcome at my house, but leave my wife alone." He said he tried to get some sleep after we left and she kept rolling him out of bed. I guess it was Monday morning and I was back at Howard Johnson's having coffee and the waitress took her break and went out back for a smoke. Two salesmen out of New Jersey came in and sat at the counter looking for the waitress. "Where is she?" they asked. I said, "She's on break and she goes over to the Exton diner for coffee. She'll be back shortly." So here she comes and takes care of the men and then she comes over to me and says, "What did you tell them?" I told her. She was ready to kill me, but I laughed.

A few days later I was in Howard Johnson's with some off-duty state police, and two uniform state police. We were at the counter. They worked part time for me, because they were allowed to have extra jobs back then. The waitress had taken their order. Then she said, "Bob, what do you feel like today?" And I said, "You look good to me," as I took hold of her and started to pick her up. And she said to the cops, "Do something." I didn't want to get them in trouble, so I put her down and ordered eggs and she laughed, for she knew I was always fooling around. We were always doing something to one another.

One day, I stopped to see Morris and left the keys in the truck, and one of the cops came in and here he had gotten the keys out of my truck. I got in, saw the keys missing, and got the other set out of my pocket and went down to the office. Then the cop pulled in and said, "I had your keys." I told him I carry two sets, and he laughed. I carried two sets of keys for a reason. Because every now and then Morris Seed or Elwood Erwin would see my truck—this was back when you could leave keys in your car or truck—and would hide each other's cars or take the keys out.

Morris, Eve, Sally, and myself would go to the Perkiomen Hotel in Collegeville to eat on Saturday nights. Morris had these pencils with a string on the end of it, and we would put them in people's button holes on their jacket or coat and if you broke the string you would have seven years bad luck. I saw a friend of mine in Downingtown one day with one on his jacket and he said, "Do you know how to get this off?" I asked him how long he had it on his jacket and he said six months, so I took it off for him.

When we would be at the hotel, they would sing "Happy Birthday" to people, and Morris and I would go around and get everybody to sing. We always had more fun than monkeys.

One night we had about 15 people in our party and the ladies went to the ladies room and Millee Miller left her purse behind and we put silverware in her purse and told the cashier, who was the owner, to watch out for her because she had their silverware in her purse. When she came outside you could hear her for a block. We were always doing something to somebody for fun.

Back in those days you could pat a girl and they would laugh at you. Today they would lock you up and throw the key away. People have no sense of humor today.

The younger people have very little sense of humor. They need to stop and look at the big picture and find God and put him back in their lives. With God, you can do anything. But without him we are nothing, believe me. I just try to live by the word, rather than go around preaching to people. Let the preacher do that. I know he has been with me on many occasions in fires, and has watched over me to come out alive. I have been trapped in fires and guys got me out—I survived.

Back in our day, they called us crazy to do what we did. After 9-11, and I mean no disrespect, they call us heroes now. But we did it because we are who we are. We helped people in trouble no matter what.

I was on the road and didn't have my radio with me. When I got back to the office, Sally said the fire whistle had been blowing for a long time. When I got to the firehouse, only one truck was out, so I took the second truck to Ship Road. When I got there the men were outside and the lady was there crying and I went up to her and she said, "My kids are inside and nobody went in after them." I said, "Don't worry, I am going in. Just tell me where you think they are, after all I helped build these houses." She said they were probably in the upstairs bedrooms. With that, I ran inside with no suit or oxygen, rushed upstairs and found the two boys, and the cat was under the bed. I came out the front door with a boy in each arm, and the cat in between the boys. The mom took them, still crying, and thanked me. I said, "Don't think badly of the others. Not everyone can run into burning buildings." I found one thing that you never forget. God gives you and every firefighter the strength to do what has to be done to save lives and get out alive. We have to always thank God for that every day. For He is with us when we need him, believe me.

Back at the office, Sally and my cocker, Candy, were waiting for me. Candy had her own chair in the office, and everybody knew that was her chair, and not to sit in it. Candy was a character in her own way. Candy was a mouser, and she could smell them no matter where they were hiding. One time, we had just got a load of Ballantine beer in, and the guys stacked the cases ten high on me. Because I am short, they liked to make me mad sometimes. So Candy was sniffing at the bottom case of Ballantine and the guys asked, "What's with her?" And I said, "There are mice in that case." And they said, "No way." I told them to take down the cases and when they got to the bottom case, there was a mouse in between the bottles. I said, "See, what did I tell you? She knows." We were over at my brother Herb's one day and Candy started digging a hole in front of Herb's house and Herb said, "What is she doing?" And I said, "There's a mouse in there." And he said, "You are kidding." "No," I said, "she knows." And then the mouse ran out and she caught it and killed it.

Also, one time in the middle of the night, she had to go out. When she came back in she threw up a mouse on the bed and Sally screamed. I cleaned it up, and we went back to bed. One thing about Candy, if you told her she was going for a ride, you made sure that you took her before you went to bed or you didn't go to sleep until she had her ride!

We had moved from Spring City to Exton in 1965, building up routes wholesale and retail. Soon I had two routes, one I took myself, and I hired Joe McGeehan to run the other route. I ran my route two days a week and Joe's route was just on Saturdays, for he worked for Mama Bell back then.

I also had a fellow named Snack, Frank Misetic, Phil Chamblin, and a couple of state cops. Back then, they could have part-time jobs as long as it didn't interfere with their jobs. I also still had Herm Walters, who worked for me in Spring City.

In between work we would go out to dinner on Saturdays with the Seeds and during the week we went to the Exton Lodge or Tee's Pub and the Pin Bowl Inn. We would have a few drinks and dance all night.

People probably won't know most of the bars I had back in the 60s. There was the Black Angus Inn, the Flowing Spring Inn, Seven Stars on Route 23, the Exton Lodge, the Pin Bowl Inn, Conestoga Tavern, Country Kitchen, Goshen Inn, Shadyside Inn, Throm's Tavern, and The Alemia Hotel. Phil got me hooked up with Goshen Inn. We would take their order over on Thursday night and stay and have dinner there and one night I'll never forget, Phil needed a partner shooting pool and asked me and I said I never shot pool in my life but I'd watch him. But he didn't take no for an answer. So I said I would try but not to expect too much. You won't believe what happened. They left me break and I ran the table and somebody said Phil brought a ringer but I honestly, never played played before. I always had a good eye when playing anything. On Friday nights we would go to Pete's, which was the Conestoga Tavern, and have dinner there then stay and drink and dance till 4:00 a.m. then back to work at 8:00 a.m. Saturday morning. I used to say I had no sympathy for drunks, so it was time to go to work. We all did our thing.

East Whiteland Fire Company had a housing and I supplied the beer and sodas for the affair and a few years later Malvern had a 75th anniversary parade and celebration and they went through 35 halves of beer and 10 halves of birch beer plus other soda. That went well into the night and a lot of us went to the Wayne Diner and raised a little hell and the owner came out and asked us to hold it down and we did.

Eventually, the fire companies started having Donkey baseball games, which turned out to be a lot of fun. You had to hit the ball, then jump on the donkey, and it would start to run toward first base. Then the donkey handler would say something and the donkey would run and then stop real quickly and over its head you would go. It got a lot of laughs and we would draw a good crowd most times. One night the leader of the crew asked if there was any place they could stay a few days, for they were in between games.

I said, "I have eight acres of grass. You can park in the field, and there is a water spigot in front of the house you can use to get water. But just don't let them get loose." They said they tie them off. They had a donkey with a foal, which was running around but staying close to the mom. I took Candy down to see the little one, and they hit it off right from the get go. They stayed four days, and we went out every day and Candy and the donkey would run around and play. It was fun to watch them and man, when it was time for them to leave, we had a problem. As they were driving off, Candy was watching and she started to cry. I told her they would be back again but she was unhappy and wouldn't eat that night. But she made up for it in the morning.

We were back to our daily workdays delivering beer and soda. Back then we delivered to bars and to homes as well. A couple weeks later the boys called and said they would be back for a few days so I told Candy they were coming back, and she ran to the front window and looked out. I told her it would be a while before they would be here. But so she made up her mind to sit at the window and wait. Two hours later they arrived. The old tail, which as you know cockers don't have very long tails, was wagging. Down from the window she came and ran to the door barking as she went. She had to wait until they got parked. After they parked I let her loose and she ran right to the donkey and they nosed one another and they had a good time. By the way, do you know what else was funny? I was a Democratic committeeman then, and it was primary election day. So I made a banner and they let me have a donkey to take to the polling place. I took the donkey down Route 30 to the firehouse. There was no problem until I went to cross the road. I watched until there were no cars in sight and started across. When we got to a solid white line in the road, that's where he parked it. All at once, all kinds of cars showed up and people were laughing because it was funny in a way. But I didn't think so. I had to get behind him and push him off the road. But I still had my fun, and one lady on the Republican side, her husband was a judge, she found out but she couldn't do anything about it. I had no trouble going back home and the boys got a kick out of it. Four days later they packed up and left, and Candy again cried.

We assisted Lionville on several barn fires. We didn't have fire hydrants back then and a lot of times we had a mile or two of hose laid to a creek or pond and they would burn for days before you would have them out. I remember a fireman from New York came down to Lionville. He said he would do better fighting a tenement in New York than we did fighting barn fires. He was probably right, with the hay and straw in the barns they tended to get mighty hot and took days to put out. We didn't get paid for our fire-fighting days. That's what we did as good neighbors and friends.

One morning I had a salesman of some kind come in and try to sell me something and I politely told him I didn't want what he was selling and he got in my face and kept pushing whatever it was. I finally said to a helper to open the door and I picked him up and threw him out the door and he landed in the parking lot. About that time Vic Abadalla was pulling up with a beer salesman and asked if it was safe to come in and I said okay. The salesman said, "I don't believe I want to make you mad," and I said, "You are right about that." In our early days I had built up a customer base with the smaller stores in the area for Frank's, for they didn't deliver out in our area at all. I built up a good soda business in that time and also had soda machines out on the street. In the meantime I also ran to fires. I carried my monitor in the truck with me so I could drop what I was doing and go to the fire.

I forget what year it was but we were fighting a big one, with the Cressman Fire Company in Whitford on Route 30. We had to halt traffic on Route 30 for several hours. We had to lay lines to the creek south of Route 30 for water, for it was an all-nighter and that is all we had to work with. It was an old turkey house. Donald McIlvaine raised turkeys for many years.

It was a three-story, wood-frame building and we had gotten too close to the building. I guess we thought we would get it under control, which didn't happen, and we had trucks too close to the building and had ladders up on the side of the building. The fire came out all three floors at the same time. Guys on ladders had to jump and run, and we could not get the trucks back in time. It burned the paint, but we saved the trucks. The fire was so bad it pushed us back to Route 30 until we could get it under control. In the meantime there were two tankers with jet fuel waiting in the line of traffic, and a young state trooper came up and said he needed to get them through, and Al said, "Turn them around and get them out of here. We have our hands full with this fire. We are the boss, you take our orders." So he called back to the station and found out Al was right.

Meanwhile back at my place, I would get a load of Frank's Beverages in every week, for I sold to stores and had vending machines. I used a lot of Coke in that time, too. I sold 200 cases of Coke a week, and at that time I was one of Sam's, who owned Coca-Cola in Coatesville, biggest customers.

He made me mad one time. They dropped a whole load of Coke down at the corner from me at the Esso gas station. I would get deliveries on Fridays, and John, my Coke driver, came in Friday morning and looked in the corner where the Coke was kept. I had two cases left. Knowing that nobody put anything in without asking me what I wanted, he said, "What do you need today?" So I told John, "Nothing until the load of Coke goes away down at the corner." John called Sam up and told him I didn't want any Coke until that load on the corner went away. Sam asked to talk to me, and he told me that it was a promotion with Esso. I said, "Promotion or not, you better do something about it or I don't use Coke anymore."

Sam said, "What do I do? I want your business." So I asked him how many cases were down there, and he said 350 cases. I told him to load them up and I would take the whole load or else.

Next thing, I looked down the corner and he sent a crew and loaded up the 350 cases and brought them up to me and unloaded in my place.

A while before this happened John Mower built the bowling alley in Frazier, and I sponsored two teams there and had a soda machine in there. It tickled me. I was in the bowling alley one day and Joey, Sam's brother from Coca-Cola was in there.

I said hi to Joey and he looked at me and kind of laughed. He said, "you sure got Sam upset." "Why's that?" I asked. And he told me Sam has a rule there now—any time Bob Reese calls, everybody jumps and gets what he needs to him. I learned a long time ago to do right by people and treat them the way you would like to be treated and that's how I live and God only asked us to do our best. In our early years in the beer business we worked hard and played hard.

On Saturday nights we would go up to the Black Angus on Route 100 to eat, for DeAngelo's owned it then, and I sold them beer and soda. They had the best prime rib around then. We got to be friends with them and not every Saturday night that we went out, but quite often, it got so they got busier all the time. We went one night and Mrs. D. said we would have to wait for a table and told us to go to the bar and she would call us. Next thing I knew, a waitress came over and said she had a table for us. Paul, the bartender, was the son-in-law, and I said to him, "What's with the waitress coming over?" And Paul said, "You are the best tipper we have and all the waitresses know it, so they fight for you." I said, "You have a lot of rich people in here." But he said, "That doesn't matter."

Al Alasiani owned and operated the diner at Route 100 and Boot Road, and later built a hotel-motel, and restaurant-bar, then got rid of the diner.

I served him beer and soda when he opened up, and he and I became friends. We would go there to eat, and he had a famous chef that cooked for the Queen of England and other famous people. He was great, and when he saw Sally and me there, he would make something special for us. One time he brought me a dish, and they looked like little meatballs, and he said to try them. I did, and they were very good. Then he told me they were sheep's balls. I said, "What?!?!" But they were very good. He made some very good dishes, and always brought us special dishes anytime we were there.

Al was a good friend, but sometimes used me. Let me explain: Sometimes at 3:00 in the morning, he would be out and get stopped for speeding or other things, and call me to get him out of a ticket, and I would take care of it.

I had joined the Lions Club, and we met up at Al's place and had dinner and our meeting, and then went up to a room to play poker all night.

At the bowling alley, I sponsored a team in the mixed league and one in the men's league. The mixed league was on Monday night, and the men's league was on Wednesday night. I started out bowling 150 and got better with practice and age, with which you always get better. Ha, ha!

I'll never forget, we were into the season and the alleys were new and for a long time there was no 300 game. One Monday we were bowling, and I got hot and was striking every time. I didn't realize I could roll a 300 game. I had eleven strikes. The manager shut down the other lanes so people could see me throw the twelfth ball for a 300, but I messed up and got a 296 instead. I think I might have made it if he hadn't stopped the other lanes, but we will never know. But we did take high game and high triple that night and it held on top for many years. When bowling was over, off to the Pin Bowl Inn for the rest of the night. We would drink and dance and drink some more. Back in those days you would drink and nobody would say too much. I used to drink a fifth of Jack Daniels and a glass of water every day. I sold beer but didn't drink it.

We went on to win the Monday night league, and we had a banquet at the Downingtown Italian Club. I was always clowning around so when the women were headed to the ladies' room, I always said, "I am going to the little girls' room," and I would open the door, and boy did the older ladies scream! From there, we went to the VFW in Paoli to finish the night out. We had suits on, and the ladies were in nice dresses. We had gotten a table and waitresses brought drinks over, and out of the blue there were two guys fighting. They hit our table and some drinks spilled on my wife, and with that a couple of guys grabbed me and said, "No, Bob." I said, "I'm okay, I won't break the place up. I just want to talk to them." I grabbed both by the collar and looked them in the eyes, and said, "I don't hit drunks, but tomorrow I will come looking for you, trust me." One knew who I was, and he told the other fellow, "In the morning, you'd better go see him. You don't want him to come after you, for you will be sorry, believe me. He can hurt you. I know."

The next morning, one fellow came to the house to say he was sorry and wanted to pay for my wife's dress, and I said, "That's alright, not necessary. Just a good thing you came. Where's the other fellow?" He said, "I think he's on his way." I was headed down the road and he waved me down, and I stopped and he said, "I was told I'd better come to you, so here I am, and I am sorry." I told him I was good with that, and let him go.

When you have a man who can throw 500 pounds over his head, you kind of think twice about messing with him, for in my day I have put guys in the hospital at times, and also shot a few trying to steal from me at gunpoint. I get a little upset when somebody points a gun at me.

I am funny that way. I have saved many lives from burning buildings, and I have put a few in the ground for pointing a gun at me. It tickled me one time, a state cop and I were inside talking, and a guy walked in and said, "Put up your hands. This is a holdup." The cop raised his hands, and I made a quick wave of the hand, which took his eye off me, and I pulled my gun out and shot him. The trooper said, "I want you on my side. I thought we were goners, but you saved the day. Thanks, Bob." The story there was he who hesitates is lost or dead.

In the early 60s, I had a salesman who had done his homework on me. He came along and wanted to sell me an ice vending machine. I said no at first, but he didn't take no for an answer. He said, "Let me put a machine out in front of your place for a time to show you what it can do for you." So I said okay, and he was right. It made me $150.00 per week at the time, which was good. He came back later and wanted to sell me more, and like a fool I fell for his deal. I was in politics at the time, and had friends in Harrisburg, so we set up an appointment and made a deal to go on the turnpike with ice machines on a handshake. But after the machines were ordered, the deal fell through. That was the beginning of my trouble. I was stuck with big ice vending boxes, which wound up costing my business a couple of years later. I hurried up and found places to put them, and I made some money, but not enough. You all know how it goes. You rob Peter to pay Paul, and it ends up not working. Anyway, I kept on plugging away at everything.

On into late summer and afternoon, the fire whistle went off for a field fire at the Atlantic Refining Plant on Route 30. The fire was heading for a storage tank, and I was first truck on the scene. The had nobody with me, for we had trouble with help in the daytime. So I pulled in between the fire and the tank and Morris Seeds was behind me and called me and said, "You'd better get out." And I said, "If I don't stop it now, it's all over." I pulled up by the pump in gear and went to work. I got it knocked down and saved the day, but we sweated it out. It was a close call, but that's what you had to do sometimes.

Back at the business, after seeing what the ice machine was doing, put in an ice-making unit, but it didn't produce what they said it would. So I started buying 300 pound blocks of ice and got a machine that chopped up ice, then we would sift the chopped ice. I had bought some storage boxes to put at gas stations. I also had a couple of guys who bought the snow for snow cones, which helped out. A lot of construction started in the area, and the union contractors needed ice on the jobs at 70 degrees, and nobody delivered in that day. A couple contractors came to me and asked if I could deliver ice to them, and I said, "You build a box to hold ice, and I will deliver to your site." Word got out, and I got calls from ten contractors working school jobs and road jobs. Diamond Ice delivered 300 pound blocks to me, and at 5:00 in the morning I would be out delivering to the job sites, and by 8:00 they had their ice on the job. Then they asked me to put soda machines on the job. I said, "I'll put them on your site, but if there's any problem with the machine, call me. Don't beat it up." They said okay. I was at Cheney College one morning. Coca-Cola had put a machine in alongside my machines, and this crane came over. A guy put a chain around the Coke machine and raised it up in the air and dropped it. It came down with a bang, and I said, "I hope you don't do that to my machine." Then he said, "Bob, you take care of us, and that won't happen to your machine. The Coke guy said you take your chances with the machine." When they say they lost money in the machines, I always took care of them.

Route 202 was being built, and Glasgow was the builder, and I got in real good with them. They were clearing the right of way, and Mike was the super. on the section from West Chester to Malvern, and one day he asked, "You are a fireman for the area, right?" I said, yes, and he asked me about burning piles of trees, and I said I would check with the chief and let him know.

Al Miller was chief, and I told him what they wanted to do, and he said as long as they had somebody there all night at the fire scene and under control, then he would let them. I got back to Mike and told him what Al said, and about that time Jim Glasgow showed up, and he looked at me and said, "You are the ice man." I said, "Yes, glad to meet you." And he said, "Bob, keep up the good work. Now about the fire, could you watch the fire? We will pay you for your time and give the fire company something, too." I said yes. I got there about 6:00 and stayed all night. I was there two nights until it went out. It was nice watching the moon and looking for the big dipper, like I did in my younger years.

I remember in the early 60s we assisted West Chester with a fire at Lasko's in town. I was first truck out of the firehouse, and later I heard Mario, who is the barber with his shop next to the firehouse, ran out and left a state trooper in the chair half clipped. His helper had to finish him up.

We had a pancake breakfast early in the day, and I'll never forget, we had an idea to put up a banner across Route 30. We got it up early when there wasn't much traffic, but it was short-lived. The wind took it down in about ten minutes, but the breakfast started a long run. Every year we had more and more people come to the pancake breakfast. So many started to come that we had a fellow build the fire company a long grill so five men could work side by side. Years later, the younger firemen didn't want to work like we did, and they gave the grill away, which was very sad. It tickled me, one day we got a call from West Chester, for they had a mushroom house in Green Hill on fire, and called for our tanker, which I took over. When I got there, their firemen got their deluge gun off their truck, and I laughed and said, "I only have 6,000 gallons of water. With your deluge gun it will take five minutes to unload the truck."

Sometime in the 1960s, Mr. Ruark came to me and asked about getting ice. His milk cooler where he cooled his milk quit on him and he couldn't get it fixed. I told him he could have all the ice he needed and could pay later or not. I just felt bad for him, for they worked hard. He had the farm and it covered both sides of Route 113 and also both sides of Dowlin Forge Road. I think he had about 300 cows. At 4:00 every day, they stopped traffic on Route 113 to drive the cows across the road to the barn to milk. Back in the early days, he made sausage and scrapple that we bought at our place back in the 30s. I always had one rule in life: Don't try to steal from me. But if you need something, and I have it, I'll gladly help you. In the summer, there was a stand on Quarry Road. He sold corn, so he would stop and get ice to cool his corn. He used to buy and sell 5,000 ears of corn a day all summer. I had eight storage ice boxes on the street. We crushed ice, and bagged and hauled it to the boxes.

Next came Mr. Yeager with Eastern Shore Charcoal. He wanted to sell to me, so I put some in my place. It was real wood charcoal, and it caught on, and the next thing. I started selling it wholesale to stores. They had built up some customers, and they turned them over to me. I started selling to stores and gas stations, along with the sodas that I sold to the stores. Back before gas grills, I sold quite a bit of charcoal, for it burns three times as hot as briquettes, and when you are finished cooking, you can put it out, and start it back up when you need it again.

I believe it was 1963, that after having the post office in our house for so many years, they built an office on Route 30 in Exton, and Mom had to, after 30-plus years, go out to go to work, which made her about 63. It tickled me, for she had a 1963 Chevy and every morning at 3:30 a.m. you could find her cleaning her car off before she went to work. It has become a first-class office, and I was glad for her, for in 1936 when they moved the post office to our restaurant, it was a fourth-class office. She worked from there, and they started a routine from there, too. She stayed on until 1965, when she retired after 30 years.

She is the only 30-year Post Master Exton has had. After she retired, the job was mine, but that wasn't for me. At that time I was a Democratic committeeman, and back then the job would go to me or somebody I chose. Martin Brittingham came to me and asked if I was going to take the job, and I said no. He then asked me if he could be in line for the job, I knew Marty and told him he could have the job. Then he asked how much it was going to cost, and I told him nothing, and he looked at me in surprise. "Nothing?" he said. "That's right," I told him, "and if anybody says anything, send them to me." So that was that. I know for a fact that for some of the postmaster jobs, people paid as high as $10,000.00 for the job.

I had the ice machines on the way and no place to put them. Bob Spaz helped me by buying one, and I set one in Goshen Shopping Center, one in Malvern, one in Phoenixville, and one on Route 724 above Phoenixville, and one in Downingtown. They took block ice and bagged ice.

So with all this going on I had three or four state troopers who would work part time, for back in the 1960s they, like everybody, didn't make that much, so they let them have part-time jobs but had to be on call if something happened. I respected their job and never took advantage of their position, but we were there for one another. It tickled me one time, in 1964 or 1965 there was a riot in Philly. The guys from the Thorndale Barracks had to go help, and they stopped in and got ice and sodas. I became good friends with Bunkie, who was a big trooper. One of the other troopers said to Bunkie, "Who do you want on your back down there?" And Bunkie replied, "Bob Reese. I can trust him. I don't know about you guys. For he is like me. We don't run, and I like that about him." That told me a lot.

Bunkie was tough, but a good man. We saw eye to eye. One thing I learned early in life: God only asks you to do your best. And I try every day to please God, and He has been there for me many times, and I know He will always be there for me, and you, too, whoever reads my book and believes you have faith, too. Bunkie used to get Morris Seed's goat at times. Morris was the J.P. and just across the tracks from me.

Bunkie would have and serve warrants in the middle of the night, then wake Morris up. Bunkie would laugh about waking him up. Bunkie and Jack Bosner and Al Taylor would come down for supper a lot. I used to get 2½-pound sirloin steaks and cook them on my charcoal grill, and back then we could all eat a whole steak. By this time I was now selling lump charcoal to stores. The Yeagers, from Maryland, got me into distributing for them. It was called Eastern Shore Charcoal, and we sold that for years, and one day they called and said their place burned down, and it put them out of business. So I found Humphrey Charcoal in Brookville, PA, and am still selling their charcoal. I lost a lot of customers to the gas grills, but the people that used my charcoal, stayed with me.

Jack tickled me. He would get all my fat, and all of Sally's fat, and eat it. He was a farm boy, too. Jack would come and bag ice for me. One day I was unloading a load of ice and Dave Jones came along and said, "Hey, Bob, I'll do that." What I was doing was bringing blocks of ice down a ramp in to the walking, and the way I was doing it looked easy. So Dave said, "Out of the way." I told him he would go on his ass, so to watch how I did it. Guess what? First block Dave tried, ass over head he went, and he said, "Looks easier than it is."

I had about nine or ten construction jobs around the area that I delivered ice to every morning. My day would start at 4:30 a.m. taking ice to the jobs. I was always on the road getting new stops.

It's funny, my wife would always say, "Why do you have to deliver the same day they call?" That's just the way I am. I like to give people the best service I am capable of giving, to all my customers. Take for example Penny, at Westtown Meat. One day I got there about 10:30 a.m., and there were other delivery fellows there. Penny said, "Here comes my man. I called at 9:00, and at 10:30, here he is. All you other guys, I call an order in and it might be two weeks before I see you. Nobody does like my man, Bob Reese."

The fire company put in a new alarm system, and we had the schools in the area connected to the alarm, using Bell Telephone lines. Every morning for about 14 days, at 8:00 on the button, the alarm went off, and off to Mary C. Howse

School we went. It was a false alarm, but you still had to run! We found out that right at 8:00 Bell used the electric power on the line. That being solved, we turned to field fires, and we had a mail car fire one morning about 8:00 a.m. I rolled in with the first truck, and there was a railroad cop there. Fire was coming out the side of the boxcar. I told the cop to get the lock off, so we could get in. But he told me he couldn't unlock the car, that Kippy had to be there to do that. So I told my men to get the bolt cutter. The cop started to put his hand on his gun. I said, "I dare you." About that time, Kippy grabbed him and told him to unlock the car and told the cop he didn't want to go up against that man, that he wouldn't win that battle. We had to remove a couple hundred bags before we got it under control. Now that we had the fire out and all bags of mail put out, we had the job of getting the mail back on the rail car. I, being first truck, was in charge of the fire. By now the Postmaster from Paoli was there, and five or six other postal employees, along with a couple union men. They started back and forth about who was going to put the bags back in the car.

They kept this up, and I saw it wasn't going anywhere, and I got up with Kippy and told him, "I have men on my truck who need to get to work, so get them moving or I will make them." A union man came up, got in my face and said when they got good and ready it would get done. I grabbed him and told him everybody was going to get up there and help load the bags, or I would be calling for ambulances to pick them up. Kippy said, "He's not one to go up against."

So everybody helped load the bags on the car and got it on the way, because I could not leave until it was back on the rail. My mom was still Postmaster, but she wasn't there. When she was told what happened, she said, "Was Bob there?" Kippy said, "Yes, and he was in charge. I thought the union and Bob were going to get into it. But I found out one of the union guys had a run-in with Bob in the beer business and told his boss, we wouldn't win. He put some guys in the hospital before."

I had to get back to work and deliver beer and soda and ice. It got so a lot of the restaurants would call and I would make 50-pound bags of ice for them. I even had places in the farmer's market who wanted me to deliver them ice.

The next big fire we had was AIW Frank Plastic Cups. Plastic fires were new in the day. I rolled in on the fire and pulled up on the right side of Route 30 with a pumper and I had a small stream to pump from. Downingtown's Ladder laid a line to me and a crew from Berwyn Ladder also laid a line and he looked at the stream and said, "Reese, you are crazy if you think you are going to pump water to two ladder trucks." I said, "Don't you worry, I'll get it done." I told my mom to dam up the stream, which was only two feet wide, and I walked up over a little hill and said, "God, you know what I need, and I am thanking you for that now." With that, I walked back to the pumpers and told them in five minutes we would be ready. Five minutes later, I put the pump in gear and pumped for 72 hours. Al Miller was chief, and he had been over during the first night and looked at the stream, and said, "I don't know how you did it, but keep up the good work." And I said, "Al, all you need is faith." Then he walked away. The fire was so big, black smoke carried full sleeves of cups as far away as the other side of Coatesville, which was 20 miles away.

Philadelphia Fire Department sent two pumpers out, and they said that if we needed them they were able to assist us. But they came to see how we handled a fire. There were two buildings within 25 feet of the fire, and we saved them. When the smoke cleared, they said, "How did you guys save those buildings? In Philly they would have burnt, too!" They were annoyed at how the volunteer fire company operated and saved lives and buildings. They said, "You guys are great. We are proud to know you and be here today. Thank you." They said they were there to watch, and told if they could help they were allowed to do so.

And back at the ranch, so to speak, my wife took care of the fort, so to speak. She kept everything moving, getting ice and beer delivered, and minding the store. At night we would do things together.

My friend Morris Seeds was a fire policeman, and would be in the middle of Exton crossroads, which was a well-known traffic hazard and the scene of a lot of accidents over the years. He would stop traffic so we could get through the crossroads with our firetrucks.

One day my friend Jack stopped to see what he had to do when he got off work as a trooper, and he saw Candy sitting in her chair, and went over and said, "Out of my chair!" Candy just looked at him. Jack said something else, and Sally got up from her desk, walked over and kicked Jack in the leg and told

*Lettie Reese, 1964*

him he better not even think it, whatever it was. He never did that again. We worked hard, but we also played hard, too.

Another of my side jobs was that I had a firewood business along with the beer, ice, charcoal, and moving, which was another story. I got a lot of wood off the road site that time they were clearing for the right of way.

About the moving bit, I had an over-the-road moving van stop one day and ask if there was any place he could stop and pick up help to unload furniture for him, since he ran loads by himself and hired help for the day to load, and at the other end hired guys to unload. In the big towns or cities, they have work pools to hire from. Out here, not so much. So I told him I'd make a couple of calls, and asked him how many men he needed. He said two or three would be good. I called fellows who worked for me and found three for him, and they got the job done. He came back to thank me, and took my name and phone number for any time he needed help in the area. He would call from time to time, and he also gave my number to other drivers that came in the area, and word got around that we moved people, too. Every now and then some women friends needed to move and didn't have money to get a regular mover, so they would ask if I knew anybody cheap, and I told them I could get them help. So my men and I would move them and when we were finished, they would ask how much, and I told them I'd take care of the help, and they would thank me. It was all part of our job to help people in need. That's what we were all about.

In my spare time during the year, I would cut and split about 80 to 100 cords a year to start. But later years I had garden centers that I supplied, and I sold wood for $15.00 a cord in the '60s. Today it is over $200.00 a cord.

Then came another fire. We assisted Downingtown at the farmer's market on Route 30 in Downingtown. On a lighter note, Malvern had a big parade and I supplied the beer, sodas, and ice. I think we went through 60 halves of beer and 15 halves of birch beer, and also tanks of Coke were used. It was a long night and I remember there was this one guy who tried to steal beer from my truck and I hollered at him to get down. He said, "I'll come down and kick the crap out of you." And another fellow said, "Do you know who you said that to?" And he said, "It don't matter." And the other fellow said, "That's Bob Reese you're going up against." He said, "You're kidding." And the fellow said, "No, and you're on your own" and with that he jumped off the truck and was gone. They were the good times back then. We firemen stuck together, and we had to, for there weren't that many back in the day. I sometimes drove a pumper to a fire, kicked the pump in gear and let another watch it while I would flag down a passerby to get back to the firehouse to bring the tanker. You worry about getting everything back later.

What was great, the fire companies banded together to make what got called the Fire Board, and it was formed to help one another so we could get enough help out to fires. The companies were Berwyn, Paoli, Malvern, East Whiteland, and West Whiteland, and we shared in expenses. The base was in Berwyn, and Buzz Harman was the operator, and he was good. He knew when to call for backup, and who to call, for back then Berwyn and Paoli were the only ladder trucks available. It worked out good, for we could run with every company if we were in the area, for it was hard to get help sometimes. As time went on, the Fire Board got better, and I know we had a better board then when the county got into it, so be it. My opinion, and I know I was right.

I'll never forget, one time in the summer, Mr. Liverside who lived off of Route 401 in a big house, had a chimney fire, and he drank a lot. He called Radnor, Berwyn, and the Fire Board, who in turn called Paoli, Malvern, East Whiteland, West Whiteland, Lionville and Downingtown. I was listening on the radio, and it turned into a circus. Radnor, Berwyn, Paoli, and Malvern were all trying to beat each other going up Route 401, and Lionville, Downingtown, and us came off of Route 100 and the road was loaded with sixteen fire trucks for a chimney fire.

I also remember back years before when we had barn fires. I remember helping with Lionville Fire Company, and the old LaFrance they used to drive. That pump could push water right through other pumps in relays. Back then all we had were creeks and ponds and swimming pools and it was nothing to have a mile or so of hose laid. And after the fires were out, we had the job of rolling all that hose up before our job was done. Also back in the early days, we would, in the summer, have three or four barn fires to fight after the farmers put up their hay and straw. They took days, sometimes, to put out. I also remember I made some of the guys mad, for they worked at cleaning and polishing a truck to go to a parade on a Saturday, and we had a brush fire on the railroad and I took the truck they washed for the parade. This was on a Friday morning. It got all dirty from the black smoke, and they were upset and gave me hell. But I told them, we bought these trucks to fight fires, not just for parades. They got over it and busted butt to get it ready for Saturday, and when the whistle went off again, I left that truck alone that time.

I know I go on about all the fires, but I am also writing our history of the company, too, and my part in it. Part of our being volunteer firemen, was that we had a picnic every year in August or September. Sometimes we had good weather, but one year, everything was ready, food and all, and it was raining pretty hard and we were in the firehouse, and somebody said, what now? And I said, "Hey, we go fight fires in rain, snow, sleet, freezing weather, so let's get the tarps off the trucks and tie them between the trees and have the picnic anyway." So we did, and halfway through the picnic it stopped raining, and the sun came out, and we ended up having a great time.

It looks like all I did was fight fires, but we still had a life. We bowled two nights a week, and went for drives every evening with our girl, Candy. She was our kid.

Every day was pretty routine: Up at 4:30 a.m. delivering ice to the jobs, checking the bars to see if they needed anything, and also buying the bar a drink while there.

One of my friends said to me one day, "Bob, you spend a lot of money in the bars." And I told him, that's how you do business. I had to do that, or my bars would buy off somebody else. I had about 12 accounts at wholesale, which helped pay the bills. Then we had the store, which we had open from 10:00 a.m. to 9:00 p.m., but closed on Mondays. Back then, that gave us time to go places and do things.

We had formed the Exton Lions in the '60s, and I was a member for a few years. Ironically, in December I got the club selling Christmas trees in front of my place, rent free, and we did well—for everybody knew me and helped us out.

Sometimes on Mondays we would go to the zoo in Philly and walk around the zoo watching the animals. We would take time on the weekends to go places and stay overnight, and go to dinner and get in some dancing, at times.

In the meantime, I also used to install TV antennas for a couple of stores. All of a sudden other stores found out about me, and I got real busy at that. I did it in my spare time, and somebody asked me when that was, and I said, "There are 24 hours in a day, and I work 16 of them most every day of my life."

I was there for anybody that needed help with anything, no matter what. I would have people come around, down and out, and I would help them out, moneywise or otherwise.

I was always stopping at the Exton Diner to grab something to eat, and at times Dee would be having trouble with a customer, and I would say, "Do you need help?" He used to tell me, "I'll take care of my corner, you take care of your corner." We would laugh about that. One morning I pulled up out front of the diner and Lois, a waitress, was cursing a truck driver out, and I walked behind her and said, "What, didn't he pay you?" And he said, "Mind your own business." I laughed and soon as she came in the diner, everybody knew what happened.

The manager at Howard Johnson's called one morning and said, "Bob, any chance you can get dry ice for me?" I said, "I'll call the dry ice company and get whatever you need." He said his freezer went up and he needed to move everything into the trailer. So I called Philly and ran down to pick it up, and brought it back to him. He said, "You saved the day." It did the job. Shortly after that, I did business with a major pipeline company, and they called at 4:00 a.m. and needed two tons of dry ice. "Can you get it?" they asked. "We had a pipeline break, and we need it as soon as possible." I called and told them what happened and they had cops meet me at City Line and escort me to get the dry ice. Then they led me all the way to the site. They used the dry ice to freeze the line so they could repair it.

Then they needed four tons of ice to bring it back slowly, or it could blow the line. I always helped them, anytime, day or night, and they knew they could rely on me anytime. That's what I am all about, helping people and making people laugh.

With me you need a sense of humor. Like I always say, "God likes a good joke. Just look at me!"

Then came the Downingtown Farmer's Market. Here we go again. Another fire, and it pretty well did it in. That was an overnighter for the Downingtown firemen. We had some house fires, and a lot of field fires in the summertime.

Franco Pipeline would buy soda, beer, and ice from me on a regular basis. Once a month they had a cookout and they started using my charcoal and really liked it. They had a chuck wagon that came all up their pipeline with beef from Texas. They always invited my wife and me, and we always enjoyed it. They were good people, and I had a lot of fun with them.

We had all kinds of beer salespeople come around. I remember Mr. Mueller from Clemen & Mueller—they sold me my Millers beer. He stopped in one day to see us, and he told Sally and me we were one of the nicest beer distributors that he had met in a long time. One thing we were taught was to respect our elders and be good to people and make them laugh and feel at home around you.

We always kept our chins up and kept going, no matter what, but 1966 would be our last year. I was having trouble meeting the bills, but we kept on fighting and finally, in August. I found a buyer, and we sold the business and building so we could get out from under debt. We came out with a few dollars, and we found a place in Meadowbrook Manor and moved there. We never had a honeymoon or vacation, so we took time and went to Myrtle Beach for a week, and it was great. When we got back, Charles Engleke a friend of mine, and I were at lunch one day, and about an hour later his wife called and said he had a heart attack and died. They were superintendents of dog shows. They did all the programming for the show, and setting up the equipment. So I said, "I'll help you out a while, until you get on your feet." I would take the big truck and drive to the shows, set up the rings, lay runners for the dogs to run around in the ring, and set up small tents when needed. It turned out to be fun and interesting. My area was Pensicola, Florida, then to Buloxi, Mississippi, and then into New Orleans, and that was a long ride. We set up in Pensicola early morning, for you had to have everything ready by 7:00 a.m. or you would be fired. I would break down there, and drive to Buloxi and work all night setting that show up. After that, I was laid over there for a week, then traveled to New Orleans, which was the big show. The dog show in New Orleans was similar to the Garden show in New York, only New York is all bred dogs.

When I got back home, I went to work at Pepperidge Farm in Downingtown, PA. I was mixing dough for the cookies, working the 3:00 p.m. to 11:00 p.m. shift. In the daytime I worked for myself, putting up TV antennas for different stores and repair shops.

William H. Murray, who I used to work for back in the '50s, called, and I did some work for him. I also did work for Rubino's TV in Paoli, Kauffman Furniture in West Chester, Moore's in Eagle, Kroeger's in Downingtown, and Tom Jones in Exton. They kept me busy, and I enjoyed making people happy. It tickled me but kind of made me upset with Dick. He always gave me the hard ones—three- and four-story jobs, which he paid me for.

One day, coming out of my neighborhood, I saw his men on a single roof house in the manor, where I lived. I billed him on Fridays to get paid, and I said, "Hey, Dick, how about giving me one of the easy ones once in a while?" Dick said, "You caught me, didn't you?" Yes, I did. Bill Kauffman would call and give me three or four jobs every week, some easy, some difficult, but I could deal with them.

I would be finished with this in the morning, then go to Pepperidge Farm from 3:00 to 11:00 p.m., and somebody asked, "When do you sleep?" I said, "About three hours a night. I am used to working sixteen hours a day, and if you sleep too long, you miss too much." Dave Jones, a friend, and also a fireman, helped me at times with antennas, and also went with me on weekends to set up dog shows. There was never a dull moment with me.

Mr. Kroper called me one day, so I stopped in and he said, "I have a job for you, and I bet you'll know what to do. Bill Hart, who is a Channel 6 TV host, is having trouble getting TV in his home. He has had many TV guys there, and nobody seems to be able to get him a good picture, and I told him I think I have the man for you. He has done much good work already for me. Bob Reese is his name, and I'll get him to call you." So I called Bill Hart and told him who I was, and he told me how to get there. He lived in a wooded area, and his antennae was up in the top of a tree. I carried, back then in the '60s, two-way radios. I gave one radio to Bill and I told him, "I am going up to the top of the tree to undo the antennae and move it around, and when you get a picture, tell me, and make sure it's clear." I loosened the antennae and turned it, and nothing. Then I raised it up a foot, then two. He yelled, "Okay." Then I tightened the pole and came down. He said, "What did you do that nobody else did?" I said, "I raised it about two feet. You see, the waves don't go straight out. They make waves up and down, and you have to hit them right. I do this all the time. I learned a while ago about the waves, and other guys just don't get it. That's why I am good at it." And he said, "You sure are, Bob, and it's my pleasure." He made a comment on his show the next day. Bill Hart was a great guy. It was good to know him, and an honor to get him a picture.

I had this antennae job for Kauffman's on High Street in West Chester. It was a 3½ story house next to the church, and God had to be with me that day. I put three ladders together with rope, and I had Dave on the ground and told him not to come up if anything happens, it's on me. I pulled everything up with a rope to do the job. People would stop and look and say, "Is he crazy?" And Dave said, "He is, believe me." I got the job done, no trouble. That's "God."

Next came another dog show up in Long Island, in the middle of the island. I didn't work at Pepperidge on Fridays, so I would leave after picking up Dave. He worked for Mehl and Latta Lumber Company in Frazier. I picked him up about 4:30 and headed out. We had to go up through New York, and I came to these big holes and couldn't miss one, and it brought Dave out of his sleep, and I said, "Sorry, Dave. I looked over, and you were out, so I decided to nap, too." He was awake, now, so after pulling over I said, "You can drive," for I knew he wasn't going back to sleep after that. We got to Long Island about 7:00 p.m., checked into the motel and ate, watched TV and hit the bed. We were up by 5:00 a.m. to set everything up by the 7:00 a.m. show time!

After we had everything set up and running, we went back to the motel and rest awhile, then we might go out and see some of the city or town, whichever it was.

We got back about 5:00 p.m., and this time we were watching the best dog for the best of show. There was one show with four German Shepherds, and the Sheltie won, and the shepherds jumped over the little one. I said, "Dave, let's go." We went in and separated them, and Dave said, "You carry them," and I said, "Are you crazy, no way." I thought they would eat us up. But somehow, when you talked to them, they backed off. You can't show fear, or they will come after you.

I forgot to mention that I had an International ¾ ton pickup from the beer business. I had Jack Newton, who had a welding shop on Route 100, make a steel rack for the back to haul ladders. He made the rack and then closed in the sides with metal also, and the back was open, and I put a wire across the back, and used a piece of canvas for the back. No door or lock. Can you imagine somebody not putting a door on the back to lock it up? At the time, I was still hauling ice for the machines, and poles and antennas, and nobody would try to steal from me, for my motto is always this: If you need something, all you do is ask, not try to steal from me, for I carry, and am not beyond shooting, which I had done a few times in self-defense. Man points a gun at me, shoot or die.

I was putting up a lot of antennas besides working at Pepperidge, where I stayed for six months. The boss came to me one night and asked how I liked working there. I told him it was okay if you can handle working four or five hours then having to hide the rest of the shift. At the time that was a normal shift. It's different now. They bust them now. I said, "I am used to working sixteen to eighteen hours a day, and at times I have been known to work around the clock for three to four days with just 15- to 20-minute naps, and then keep going. I have been called a lot of things over the years, but never lazy." After Pepperidge, I stepped up my antenna business to the point that I was using fifteen to twenty Winegard antenna in a week. Alma, in Morristown, was my supplier of antenna, and they said one day they were sending me on a free weekend to Grossner's in New York on Winegard. We had to attend meetings in the mornings and had afternoons off and floor shows at night. While I was there, I signed up for 100 antenna, which I bought over the next five weeks. While at Grossner's, on Saturday night there was a comedian onstage, and Sally and I were sitting at the front table. He started off with a joke, and before he said the end line, I came off with the end, and he started a second, and I came up with that, too. Now I think I annoyed him, but he tried again, and again I finished his joke. Then he came down and said, "Would you like to come up and do my show, and I'll sit and have a drink with your wife?" I let him finish, and he came down and sat with us, and told me, "You are good. You have a future." But I said, "No, I just make people laugh."

It turned out to be a nice weekend, and we enjoyed that stay. It was all you could eat, so Sally was in her glory. She had two and three helpings at each meal. Then it was back home and work. I was still doing the ice boxes, selling hardwood charcoal, and doing antenna. Then came a fellow along and asked me to help him install automatic fire systems in restaurants and hotels. So you see, I kept busy besides weekend dog shows. You also might think I was dull, but no. I was the life of the party a lot of times.

I believe it was 1968, on the southern side of New Orleans, we were at the armory that year, and a girl had her dog in the ring. It messed in the ring, and I went in to help her out, and she was bent over, and guess what? Bob is a patter, and I did. After that, I went back in the back where the army guys were, and one said, "Hey, Bob, guess what? You were on national TV when you patted that girl." I said, "You are kidding." He pointed to the TV, and it was on, and he said, "That is national TV." When I got back home the next week, I was at the little store on Boot Road, and a buddy of mine saw me, and he said, "Hey, Bob, I saw you on TV patting that girl, and I said, he's at it again." A couple weekends later, we were in Winston Salem, North Carolina, at a show, and at the end of the show with the run off, we would guess what dog would win. There was a girl there with a Scotty, and they were in the run off. The girl was well endowed and the judge was a retired Chicago fireman, and I told them she was going to win, and they laughed at me. But she won, and I was taking down the fencing and the judge was doing his paperwork. I said, "Sir, can I ask you a question?" He said, "Yes." I said, "I am a fireman also, and I would like to know what kind of dog she had?" He broke out laughing and said, "You are right. So be it."

Back home, while doing antenna, I had a job in Coatesville for a fellow who had a jewelry store. It was a big, three-story house, and when I got there, I looked at the job, and he asked me if I could get him reception, for it was close to Lukens Steel, and it was hard to get a picture in the area. I looked around and said, "Somehow I'll get it done for you." I had to put a ladder up to one roof and one more ladder to get where I needed to go. In the meantime, he asked me about painting a couple of dormers while I had the ladders up. He told me somebody wanted to charge him $400.00 to go up and paint them. I said, "Go get the paint, and I'll do them for $50.00 apiece." So he did, and I painted them after I did the antenna, which got him good reception, and he was pleased. In between antenna and fire systems, there was still the ice boxes to fill and charcoal to deliver, but we still had time in our busy life to go to dinner and go dancing. Sally, at one time, worked at Deluxe Check Printer, and they always had a Christmas banquet, and we had fun.

One weekend, we were off to Cranton, Rhode Island, for a Newfoundland dog show, and Sally and our Candy, my black cocker spaniel, went along. We were on the third floor at the hotel and went down in the elevator to the first floor. The door opened, and standing there were two big Newfoundlands, and Candy looked at me, and I said, "It's okay. They won't bite." As we walked past them I was laughing, but I don't think Candy thought that was funny.

One year, Astrad took us to the Garden show, and we stayed at the hotel across the street from the Garden. In the morning we had breakfast and started out the front door, when a guy on drugs came through the door and headed right at Astrad with a knife in his hand. Lou was on one side, and I was on the other side of her, and I said, "Lou, you hit him low, and I'll go high and knock the knife out of his hand." That's what we did, and I had him on the ground, and the cops came and took him away. Astrad was shaken up a bit. She said, "Thanks, Bob. I don't know what I would have done without you two." We were there to see the show and trump up some business. Later, she said, "No wonder you are such a good fireman back home. People say you run into burning buildings with no regard for your own life." And I said, "There is a reason, for I have 'God' with me, so I don't have to worry." I have had a few close ones.

I took on another fire extinguisher company in Philadelphia, to teach a buddy of mine, Jim Cole, the ropes of installing systems. I always worked with Big Frank, as he was called, and Fidelity Fire, by the job. I would check the job and tell them what I would charge, and that's how I got paid. I would install the system, and do the drawing and paperwork, and guarantee it to be approved, or I would do it over. I never had to do any over. You do things right the first time. I took Jim on the job and showed him how to do things right. For in everything, people like to cut corners. Not me. Never will that happen.

Big Frank had a job at the Trenton Railroad Station for me to do. I laid down for a nap one afternoon before heading out, and the phone rang, and the man asked if I was Mr. Reese, and I said, "Yes." Then he said, "I am so and so with the FBI. Do you have a job at the Trenton Railroad Station?" I said, "Yes." He asked if I carried a gun. I said, "Yes." He said, "Good. My man will meet you out front at 5:00 p.m. and take you and your equipment inside, and while you are working, if anybody comes at you, shoot to kill." I said, "I have no problem there." There had been a train robbery the night before, and they shot several robbers. I had no incidents. I worked half the night with no trouble, and back in Philadelphia, where Big Frank's office was, three of his men had their vans broken into, and they asked me if I had any trouble. I said, "No, there is no door on the back, so they think there can't be anything there to steal." I laughed at them.

I had a job in the state prison in Newark, New Jersey, and was there for two days. I had a helper with me. We were working in the kitchen drilling in the hood and heard some noise coming from the ceiling. I called the guard, and here they found a prisoner in the ductwork above us.

From there I had a job on North Broad Street in Philadelphia that took me three nights, for I could only work about four hours a night. When I was all finished except for hooking up the shut-off valve to the gas, I had to go down in what they called a basement, but it was dirt and just a walkway, to the shut-off valve.

As I was walking I sensed something watching me. I shined my light around, and there was one of those rats that came off the ships. He was big. I pulled out my gun and shot him. He was twice as big as a cat, no lie. I went upstairs, and there were people working in the kitchens. They were all outside and wondered what happened.

It was getting a little cooler now, so I was out cutting firewood again, for I had two customers. Each took 400 cords per year. That gives you good exercise and keeps you in shape. In the meantime we still got about two to three fire calls every day.

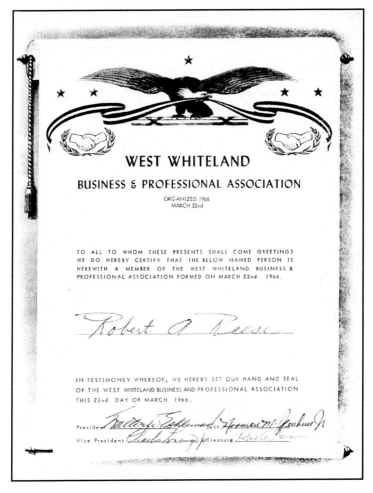

*West Whiteland Business & Professional Association certificate (March 22, 1966)*

# THE 1970s

Sally saw a shop in Marchwood Shopping Center, where a lady had a shop where she would buy and sell baked good. She closed up, and Sally wanted to see about that.

We looked into it and rented the shop then went to Philly to find cases, which I found, bought, and set up. We bought an oven and mixer, refrigerator, and freezer. We went to Reading to Shoffer's Bakery and started buying their goods and selling them. One day I said, "I can find somebody to show me how I can make better products than this." So I went out to a few shops looking, and I was in one off of Route 202 talking to a fellow and went back home. A couple of days later, this old man walked in and said, "I saw you at the shop the other day, and I came looking for you." He told me he was listening to me and his boss talk, and that I was looking for somebody to teach me baking and things. He said, "If you are willing, I'll come to work for you and teach you, for I've seen something in you that I haven't seen for a long time. You have that get up and go drive that I like." So he went to work and taught me the fundamentals of baking. We sat down and figured out what ingredients to buy, and I said, "It takes the best to make the best." He lit up and said,

"I am going to like working with you." We got started. Fred was his name. He and I hit it off, and away we went. Pat DeHaven came to work for us. She worked the store. Fred taught me how to do sticky buns, Danish, éclairs, cream puffs, and cakes—the cakes I helped bake at first.

I went out after a few days and started building a wholesale route. We made donuts, Danish, and sticky buns, and I sold them to stores. I got in with Paoli Hospital and sold to them—I was on their doorstep by 5:30 a.m. every morning. I had 15 stops, and we made 60 dozen sticky buns, 60 Danish, and 300 dozen donuts every day. Fred would decorate and put in the case 15 to 20 cakes a day, and the girls would write the names on the cakes. Back then, for school classes, parents would come in for cupcakes for the whole class, which could be 24 to 30 cupcakes. One day, after watching Fred decorate for a while, as I was leaving I said, "Don't forget, we need at least 20 cakes decorated today." He said, "Okay." When I got back from delivering, I looked in the case, and there were five cakes. I said, "Pat, where are all the cakes?" She said, "Fred said tell Bob it's time. It's up to you, Bob." And guess what? The first one wasn't that pretty but somebody bought it, and the next came out pretty good, and the rest was history. Back then was not like today. You had yellow cake and chocolate cake. And that was it!

Joe Lamont came in one day and talked me into taking on his coffee, and that turned out great after a while. People saw that we opened at 6:00 a.m., and we built the coffee and donut business up. I was using eight cases of coffee a week.

Lasorda's had Marchwood Tavern, and we got really friendly with them, and after we were open a while, when the Dodgers were in Philly playing ball, they would come to the tavern to eat. Then guess what?

After they closed the tavern, it would be about 2:30 to 3:00, they came down, and by that time we had Danish, sticky buns, and donuts ready. I met all of them, but that was in the '70s, and now, as I am writing this book, it is 2014 and I am 83 years old, so don't expect me to name them all. I remember Jimmy John, the pitcher, Tom Lasorda, and a few others. In fact, a lot of them said I made the best donuts, and they eat all over the country. Then there were the Lasorda brothers— Eddie, Harry, Smokey, and Morris—later we got to be good friends, and on down the road at times they would come down, and if my help didn't show, they would stay and help out.

One day I was in the back working and this lady came and wondered why we didn't have a full sheet cake in the case for her. She got a little loud, so I went out to see what was going on, and she said, "I need a full sheet cake for tomorrow, and you don't have any in the case." I said, "Lady, if you need a full sheet cake for tomorrow, tell me and I'll have it ready first thing in the morning." She said, "What do you call first thing?" I said, "Lady, we work all night. It will be ready by 6:00 a.m. Is that good enough for you?" She said, "Really?" And I said, "Yes." Then she told me she worked for National Liberty Insurance Company, and her job was to have a birthday cake for everybody, and they had 3,700 employees. I said, "Well young lady, if you have that many, you came to the right place, for if you have a lot in one day, tell me and I will deliver to you." She said, "You will do that?" I said, "I sure will. You let the girls know what you need, and we will make anything you want." That worked out real good. I would deliver many times after that, and after that Pepperidge Farm came for cakes, Pillsbury, and a couple other businesses. I would take care of all my customers with respect. We made all scratch cake. We made close to a pound cake. When we made wedding cakes, when they cut them, they might not have even a handful of crumbs.

We baked and froze our cakes as soon as they cooled down, some right in the freezer. Cake was one thing that came out better than anything else.

It was nothing for us to do 55 cakes a day, but not today, with all the grocery stores into it. If you want good cake, still find a bakery to get your cakes. It's more money, but the old saying goes, "You only get what you pay for." And that still goes more so today. I'll never forget going into Thanksgiving my first year, we brought in enough product to make 900 pies. We only had orders for 13 pies two days before Thanksgiving, and Fred said, "Are you a gambler?" I said, "Yes." So we went ahead and made 900 pies, and guess what? We had, on Wednesday night, only 12 pies left.

*Lasorda Brothers*

My brother, Earl, was the manager of the Holiday Inn in Lionville, just north of us. I started delivering to them donuts, Danish, and sticky buns. Edna was running the wedding part of the operation, and she had us doing wedding cakes and birthday cakes. Also, we made puff shells for luncheons. Earl would tell all the help to let him know when I was in the building, because I used to chase the girls around. I really did things to get him upset, for when we were young he used to pick on me to get me in trouble. But I didn't need his help, I got in enough trouble on my own. One time I went up for a late lunch, and there was only one table of fellows in the back, and the hostess put me at a single table in the middle of the dining room. So I got up, and put two tables together, and she came back to see what I was doing, and I told her not to mind, I had it covered. I took all the salt and pepper off the table, then here comes the waitress. "Bob, what do you want today?" she asked. I said, "You will do." She said, "Hold that thought, and I'll be back." She took care of the other table, then came back and said, "I'm ready." Up on the table I put her. About that time, out of the corner of my eye, I saw Earl in the doorway. He stopped, looked, and left, knowing what I would say if he came over. She probably got hell after I left. I was always the one you don't dare do something to, for I would do whatever, believe me.

Back in the '70s, at Christmastime, we would make 3,000 pounds of cookies. Every morning at 4:45 a.m. I was on the road delivering. My route was into the Exton Mall, down to Frazier, on to Paoli, over into Malvern, then to West Chester, then Downingtown and Thorndale, and back to Lionville and Marchwood, and back in time for bringing bread out of the oven at 7:15 a.m. By 8:00 a.m. customers were coming for hot bread and rolls. I had gotten Sal and Jennie Baldio, at the Little

Store, to sell my donuts, sticky buns, and Danish. I built the business up over a couple of years.

I also had a lady and her son come in and buy some things. They were standing out front of the store, so I took a break to step out to talk to them and asked her where they were from, and she said Washington, D.C., and her son was going to Church Farm School. She was eating a Danish and she said, "This is really good." One day, about a week later, I got a phone call and it was the lady from D.C. She asked if they ordered things could they come pick them up. I said, "Yes, and you are . . . ?" And she said, "I am one of President Nixon's secretaries, and they liked what you made." So they ordered a lot and sent a limo to pick it up. About every two weeks they would call, that being a feather in my cap, so to speak.

---

Doctor Willie Weicket and I date back to the 1970's when he and his wife opened a cheese shop in the Parkway Shopping Center and I was delivering donuts and pastries next door to a deli that was there. They contacted me at the bakery and I sat down with them and they asked if I could make a loaf of french bread for them and I said I could, so that is how things started with us.

We have had Cocker Spaniels all our married life. Candy was our black Cocker Spaniel and we were going to Dr. Gasser in Malvern at the time. Candy died in my arms on the way to the vet and Dr. Gasser didn't cremate animals; so he sent us to Dr. Willie who owned West Chester Veterinarian Medical Center in West Chester, Pa.

Shortly after Candy died we had gotten another Crocker named Ginger who after a few years got ear trouble. Willie would have to operate, but he wasn't sure how to do the operation. He had a friend who was a vet in Colorado and he took it upon himself to go out to see him and learn how to do the operation. He did the operation on Ginger and it turned out good.

We have gone to Willie ever since and we had Joy, Abbey, Lacey, and Lindy over the years and Willie took care of them all. He loves animals and now has a hospital fully equipped to handle most cases.

He can take x-rays and has wading pools for the dogs or cats. He also has a 24-hour clinic with nurses and doctors there 24 hours a day.

---

I think it was in '73 I sold the bakery to a guy. He took over and soon didn't want to work that hard, so he stopped delivering. Then Sal called me and said that I got him in trouble and had to help him. I had him selling 200 dozen donuts on a Sunday morning, so I could see why he was upset. I stopped over and looked in the paper and found a fellow with everything we needed, so we loaded it up and set up in the basement. I went to work and it was history. I built their donut business up to 300 dozen on Sundays. I also built them a wedding cake business. On a Sunday I would make 10 dozen sticky buns, 15 dozen muffins, and snowflake rolls, and 2½ pound twist breads.

I got a little ahead of myself here, and I am backing up a minute or two. I forgot some

*Lacey and Lindy*

*Sally and Ginger*

*Lacey, Lindy and horses*

things. While I had the bakery, or we, Sally and I had, Burroughs Corporation came to us in the '70s and asked if we could make a cake for their opening of the computer age. We built a cake to look like their computer, and we went on from there with them. They built a hotel for the school to teach their computers, and Saga Foods had their food service, and we got on board with my donuts, Danish, sticky buns, and dinner rolls, and I had a good run with them.

I forgot to mention that back when Agnes hit in the '70s, I still had state cops as friends, and I would make a lot of bread, rolls, and pastry, and send it up with them to help out.

Still being a fireman, when we had big fires, I would send things out to the fires. I remember one morning while I was delivering, after I left the Paoli Hospital, I saw the flames from Fisher's Feed Mill in Malvern and stopped at the firehouse. I had Tom Supple's order in the van, which was about 25 dozen donuts, sticky buns, and Danish, and Tom was there with the Goshen Fire Company. I told him, "I'll go back and get more for your store." He said, "Okay." I know I talk a lot about the fires that we had back in our day. It's so the younger guys can know what we did in the old days. They need to learn what it was like. One day in at firehouse they got a new pumper, and I was looking at these trucks, and I said, "Where were these trucks when we needed them? We had an old Dodge pumper and an old open LaFrance pumper to fight fires.

Back at the bakery in the '70s, when Pillsbury was in Downingtown: they came to me and wanted to buy my pie crust recipe for $10,000.00. I said, "No way, for I would have to pay you to use my recipe." They said, "Yes." So I said, "No." End of story.

Back to the Little Store: Every day I would make 20 donuts, 4 dozen Danish, 3 dozen sticky buns, and 6 dozen muffins. Then on Saturdays, I made 50 donuts along with the other things, and bread and rolls. Jennie also did catering, and I would do trays of miniature cream puffs, éclairs, Danish, sticky buns, and brownies, and I mean a lot at times.

Also while I was doing all of the baking, I still had my charcoal business and was still cutting firewood. When I got finished baking, I would go out and cut four cords of wood every day, for I sold 800 cords per year. I know I am crazy, and Sal said one day, "I know what you do, and I would never try to keep up with you." I said, "Hey, we grew up working, so you keep going."

Tom Lounge ran the Radnor Hunt Club's kitchen, and he got birthday cakes and wedding cakes off of me. On race day in May, he would get 8 to 10 sheet pans of brownies and pastry for the show. Come one November, he stopped in and said, "Bob, I need pumpkin pie for 500 people. Can you do that?" I said, "Sure can, Tom." I made up dough and rolled out and filled sheet pans, which after I baked I cut 54 to the sheet pan, so I did 10 pans for him, along with cream puffs and éclairs. Tom would stop or call about 9:00 a.m. and need things for lunch, and I would always take care of him.

One time, I'll never forget, he forgot a birthday. He called and asked, "Bob, can you do a cake?" He needed it in four hours. I said, "Okay.

I baked it off, then tried to cool it down in a hurry. I iced and decorated it, and was heading to deliver the cake. I had a station wagon at the time and had the cake sitting alongside but a little behind me. The light changed as I got there, and I hit the brake harder than I wanted. When I looked back the top layer was sliding, so I turned the cake around and it slid back in place, and I sat there laughing. What else was there to do?

Backing up to when I had Sally's bake shop: One day a little lady came in on a Saturday morning all upset and rightly so. I asked If I could help her, and she said her daughter was getting married, and they had gotten a cake from another bakery, but when they delivered the cake, they dropped it and would not do anything about it. I said, "Where is it at, and what colors are on the cake, so I can take the icing to fix it up for you?" I followed her to the hall, took the cake apart, and redid the whole cake to what she wanted. When I was finished, she said, "How much do I owe you?" I said, "Nothing—enjoy!" She hugged and thanked me. That's old school, older generation, but not today and that's sad.

Back at the Little Store, Jennie did catering. It got so we had one or two wedding events every other weekend. I would do the regular things for the store, and get the wedding cakes finished and delivered. I also made trays of sticky buns, Danish, cream puffs, éclairs, and brownies, and for the store I made one to two sheet pans of brownies a day. Going into Thanksgiving I would work around the clock for three days, with a catnap at times. I would roll and put together and bake 1,100 pies for Thanksgiving Day, and then on Thanksgiving morning make 50 donuts, 10 dozen Danish, 5 dozen sticky buns, 21 dozen éclairs, and muffins for the morning.

After all that was done, I would do 100 loaves of 2½ pound twist breads, and 150 dozen snowflake rolls, and everything was sold by 11:00 a.m., and I was done. I had to get some sleep after that. I did all of the above by myself, and Sal used to look at me and say, "I don't know how you do it. I wouldn't even try to keep up with you." Then we were into the Christmas holidays, and I made up a lot of trays for Christmas and New Year's, too.

In 1974 and 1975, Sally and I had been on vacation in Myrtle Beach, and met people who had a gas station down there. We got to be friends with them, and they talked me into going down and setting up a bakery. So off I went, and after I got things set up, we moved down and opened the bakery. It went well during the summer but was dead in the winter, so we came back up until spring, then went back down, only in 1975 in the middle of the season. Me and the partner had words, and it was downhill after that. I got mad and walked out, and lost the money I had put into the bakery.

While I was still there, a fellow from a big bakery in Virginia called me and asked, "Mr. Reese, are you by chance a Dutchman?" I said, "Yes, a Pennsylvania Dutchman." He said, "I thought so, for I grew up in Reading, PA. I also told my boss, for somebody brought in Danish, sticky buns and donuts of yours, and I said, give that man time and money, and he will make you a believer." So, before I left Myrtle Beach, I started up a Mother Kitchen cheese route in the south. I got in with Swiss Colony Cheese Shops at the time. I got into a few of their stores, and I would go in and stay there a day to sample the cheesecake, and I made a hit with the owners, and they came down to North Carolina to meet me. This happened after a few months of doing business with the stores. They gave me an order to fill, and I went back to New Jersey, where the cheesecakes were made, and got off with Al, (I forget his last name), but anyway, after all was said and done, he wanted to talk to them. I gave him their number, and he talked to them and tried to cut me out, but the Swiss Colony people said no to him and got back to me. They told me that if I ever had anything they could use, to call them, for they liked doing business with me.

Then we moved back home to Pennsylvania and after a while went back to the Little Store. After I had left and went to Myrtle Beach, they had somebody who I had taught working for them, and things went downhill. I got back in there, and so, as I was back, it picked back up. I heard somebody say one day, "Bob is back. You can tell how he makes things."

Before I forget, back in Myrtle Beach I used to go to a chiropractor. One day, just like the South, I had an appointment and when I got there, there was a sign on the door that read, "Gone Fishing." He didn't even call me. After him, another young fellow took over his operation. I went in one day, and knowing the walls were thin, I said, about the time he was going to crack my back, "I'm going to holler." He said, "Don't. I have new patients out there, and they will run out the door."

Now that I was back at the Little Store, I was having more trouble with my back, I thought, but it turned out to be my hip. Doc Berry had been taking care of me for a while, and in '78 I was there one day and said, "Doc, you aren't doing me any good. Do you have an x-ray machine?" He said, "Yes." He took an x-ray and I went home. He called and said, "Bob, get your butt back down here now. I'll wait on you." I walked into his office and he took me back and slapped the x-ray up in the viewer and said, "How are you even walking?" I said, "With a lot of pain."

Dr. Franfarra was head of Paoli Hospital then, and I called him, for I had done him a service a few years before. He got me in with Eagle's doctors at the time. So I got a new hip put in. You have to know me, I'm an old farm boy and was able to throw 500 pounds over my head. Trust me, many people found that out the hard way. I put a few guys in the hospital at times. So anyway, I got the hip in and asked Doc how long it would take to heal, and he said, "Six months to a year, it's all on you." A few days later a nurse brought in a walker and I said, "What's that for?" She said, "It's for you." I asked where the doctor was and she said he was out in the hall. I said, "Go get him." He came in in a huff and said, "What's your problem?" I pointed to the walker and said, "That is your problem." He looked at me, puzzled and I went on. "You see that window over there?" He said, "Yeah." I said, "Well, the walker is going through that window, and you will follow." He turned to the nurse and said, "Get him crutches," and ran out of the room.

I didn't tell him, but 4 weeks from the day I was operated on, I stood 16 hours and did 7 wedding cakes, and delivered them, along with the regular things for the store.

In the meantime, Sally and I had been going to Good Samaritan Church in Paoli, on the side of the hill, for some time, and one Sunday a visiting preacher from North Carolina was speaking, and at the end asked if anybody wanted to give himself up to God. I stood up along with some others, and all of a sudden it hit me like a sledge hammer, and down on my knees I went, and all at once peace came over me. What a feeling that was. Thank you, God. I have been with him ever since. I know He's always there looking out for all of us. From that day until this day as I am writing my book, God was always with me, and I with him.

Back in the day, I was always busy. I had the charcoal, cut firewood and baked, often baking 10 to 12 hours. I would leave there and go out in the woods and cut four cords of wood every day. Then I would go home and cook supper for Sally, my wife, and rest until time to take a nap. I slept, on the average, three to four hours a day, but no longer, for I always said, "You sleep too long, you miss too much."

At the Little Store there was a basement, and how I pulled off doing a cake for Jennie's birthday one day, I don't know, but I got it done. I made the cake to look like a 747 airplane. It had a four-foot wingspan and was eight feet long. I used a 4 x 8-inch piece of plywood to put it on. We had a garage door downstairs and double doors going into the store. I remember a friend came in, and he flew 747s out of Philadelphia, and he walked around the cake and said, "Bob, I don't know where you get your info, but that cake is a right-on piece of work." After that, down the road, Bill Cockerham was Chief of Police in Malvern and a good friend. He was retiring, so I made a cake and it looked like a policeman. It stood 52 inches tall, and when we carried it into the Downingtown Inn Motor Lodge everybody thought it would fall over. But I had a platform inside with pipe to support it.

Then for the next project I did a cake to look like the church of the Good Samaritan Church in Paoli, PA. Wally, who was the preacher and a good friend, was retiring, and that cake was about 180 pounds. Wally said, "Bob, you made an exact replica of the church without a drawing." I said, "When you have God as your boss and teacher, you can do anything." Wally said, "Bob, you got it." I said, "I thank God every day for hitting me over the head that morning. God is good, God is great." He said, "Amen to that." While everybody was raving about the cake, for it was bigger than they had anticipated, Father Wally said, "Bob, you made the cake, you have to cut it." So I did.

I always liked doing big cakes that nobody else would take. Back in 1978 I made a wedding cake for a ceremony in South Carolina. I put the cake together right at the Armory, in Union, South Carolina. It took me three days. I used 42 sheet pans of cake, and the cake was close to 600 pounds. There were 4,000 people invited to the reception. It tickled me, as each day the local paper would take pictures of me and the cake as I was putting it together.

They watched each time and asked questions like, "How do you get a big, round cake out of sheets of cake?" I have a string and if it's a 30-inch round, I measure 15 inches and put sheets together and draw the circle out and put it together, and so on. The base of the cake was four feet square.

The florist came in and said, "You have been in this town three days, and your picture has been in the paper every day. I've been here 25 years and never had my picture in the paper." I had to laugh, for this was the biggest wedding cake to that date to be made in Union, South Carolina.

I tend to skip around a bit anymore, for I get going on something, then I remember something that happened before that, I need to tell, so bear with the old fellow. My daughter says I am older than dirt.

On into Christmastime. This one year, we had a call to assist East Whiteland Mehl and Latta Lumberyard. It was Christmas Eve, and the temperature was about five degrees. I rolled in and laid double line from there to the hydrant. I always connected hard hose, that way I would get good water pressure to the fire. A while later, while pumping, the man from the water company came along and looked at what I had hooked up and said the other trucks down the line weren't getting any pressure or water, and he said, "Now I know why. You are stealing their water." I laughed and said, "I can't help if they don't know how to hit the hydrant to hook up the hard lines."

In the meantime, just a few days before this fire, John Parkson, who was an officer was to a school. He said, "We need to take all the hose off the beds of the trucks twice." So after this fire, we had all the hose off all the trucks. Back at the firehouse on Christmas morning, we had to repack the hose. Then later on Christmas, we got another call from Downingtown, and that turned out to be the Downingtown Motor Inn. We were there all night and later into that afternoon and back at the firehouse. This was now the second time in two days we had all the hose off the trucks. I, being a smartass, said, "Hey, John, we don't need to unload for another year," and the guys laughed.

    I guess by now you wonder why I talk a lot about the fires we had. I would hope I am showing the younger firemen in our company what we went through and how we built the company from ground zero—just two old fire trucks—up to today with all this big equipment. Where were these trucks when we needed them? Yes, we were a different breed than the younger guys, I know. Most of us ran into buildings not thinking about our lives but about saving others. That's what we were all about, and we watched out for each other. When we went into burning buildings, we knew we were not alone, trust me. God was always there watching out for us, and don't ever forget that. We have to, as firemen, praise God every day for protecting all of us. I always say, "With God we can do a lot, without him we are nothing." I hope you understand where I am coming from.

---

    It was about two years ago I had trouble with my right shoulder and went to Dr. Odgers in Exton, and he x-rayed me and said I have four bones that have deteriorated, and I need to put a complete shoulder in, and in October be operated on me Thursday afternoon, and I got back in my room about 9:30 p.m., and Friday morning at 8:00 a.m. he came in and asked how I felt, and I raised my arm up like nothing was wrong, and he said I must have done a good job. And he thanked me and said, "Please take it easy for a few weeks." And I said, "I'll try." I did for one week, and I was back on the rolling pin making pie shells and kept on going. You see, I don't have time to be sick.

---

I taught a fellow my baking, which I find only some rubs off on them—they only learn a little. They think they know it all, and I had to laugh. After I built up a cake business, they decided I didn't know how to decorate anymore, and that got to me. In the meantime, while I was working one Saturday, Sal started asking questions about what to do, for they took on feeding 150 people for Sunday morning breakfast, and I knew he wanted me to help. Then Sunday after working all night, he was asking about how to do something, and I said, "You want me to go and help?" Sal said, "You worked all night." I said, "What's that got to do with what you need now? I know you need me, so I'll go help." It was a good thing I did. They did a good job catering, but cooking breakfast is a different ballgame, and I helped them through that. Shortly, I left there for a while, and I wasn't doing anything. Sally said that Deluxe Checks, where she worked, was hiring short-term people to help out with a promotion they were doing for a bank. So I went and helped for a time, and when it was over, we all got laid off. But the boss said, "I would like to keep you, but I can't. You worked circles around the others."

Then one day I heard about a good baker job at Cabrini College, so I went down and applied for the job. It was Seilus

*Church Cake*

*Fire Company Cake*

*Doll Cake*

*Pan Am Cake*

*Wedding Cake*

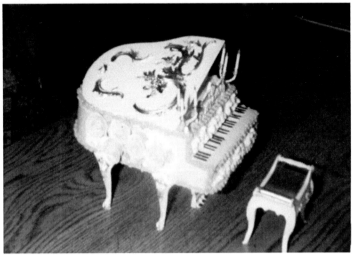

*Piano Cake*

*Union S. Carolina Wedding Cake*

*Police Officer Cake*

Food Service, and I got the job, and a buddy of mine said, "They hired you and they didn't know." I said, "It only took two days, and it was too late." I play jokes on people, but I am harmless. If you get in trouble or need help, I'm there for you. With me around, you're safe, trust me. There were guys that found out you better treat a lady with respect, or else I would tend to them, and have, many times. I like to kid and play tricks, but not harm anyone.

Bill Hale was my boss, and he asked, "What do you do as far as cooking and baking?" About that time a bread man came through the door and saw me and said, "Okay, no. You have got to be kidding me." He looked at Bill and said, "Did you hire him?" Bill said, "Yes." The driver said, "There goes my pastry business with you." Bill said, "Why?" He said, "You don't know him, then? He's the best donut, sticky bun, Danish, cake, and pie-maker around, and all I'll be hauling in here is bread, trust me. You will find out." Bill looked at me and said, "Is that true?" I said, "Yes, I have that reputation. I used to take stops off of him years ago, and he never forgot me."

So I started making my sticky buns, Danish, and pies. I also did breakfast for about 75 when I got there, and I would talk to the kids. It got so I made anything they wanted. We had omelets on the menu once a week, but after I was there a while, I had a big grill to work with. It was ten feet long. After a while, the kids got used to this crazy old guy, and more came to breakfast. I was cooking for about 125 to 150 in the morning. After baking, the nuns got so they would send over and ask for me to do a luncheon or special dinner for them, and they would ask me to make things for them. I enjoyed doing special little dinners for them. I kidded with them, and they kind of got used to me, but one time I did something and the nun said, "Bob, you are crazy, but we all love you."

I am one always to be early wherever I worked I would eat in the parking lot waiting for Bill, and one day he came back to where I was working and threw a key on the table and said, "I am not getting up any earlier for you, for the guard tells me how early you get here."

Two things about me: Time doesn't bother me, for I gave them plenty, and money doesn't bother me, either. I always liked being there for the kids, and also liked to see them grow into fine ladies and gentlemen, God bless them. What also tickled me was Eric, who was the assistant manager. Later he said to me that he hadn't wanted to hire me, but he thought I was too old to do the job, but he said, "You know how to work and get things done. I am amazed at what you can do." I was there about three years, and I guess my second year I was working back on my table, and three fellows from the home office came in, and Bill took them over to see the nuns. He said they were going over to talk about a new contract. About 30 to 45 minutes later they came back, and I looked up, and Bill and the three were heading toward me, and they said, "We got the contract no trouble and all on account of you. The nuns talked about you and how you have inspired the students and how, since you have been here, their grades have gone up."

Soon after, there was a nun celebrating 50 years of being a nun, and guess what? They were having a dinner for 175 people, and they said I had to cook the dinner, but I said to Bill, "Your two cooks went to school." Bill said, "They said for you to cook dinner." I was busy that weekend. I made sticky buns, Danish, cream puffs, and éclairs, and also a big cake for the occasion, and they also invited my wife. I was taking a break and went out to get a cup of coffee. My wife was sitting with three nuns, and they only said, "Mrs. Reese, you've got to be a saint." I laughed after I got past them. To this day, which is June 14, 2014, I think back, and it was a fine time in my life, working there and seeing the students, and how they enjoyed the things I made for them. I also started making breads and rolls, which they enjoyed. In fact, they raved about them! Cabrini College is a beautiful college, and I believe a good college to go to.

The nuns were great, and when they heard I was leaving, they came and tried to talk me out of leaving, but I told them we had decided to move to Smyrna, Delaware.

The irony of moving to Smyrna, and I have to laugh, was I really didn't leave, for Sal called me from the Little Store and asked me to come up. He said, "I need you, for the baking part fell off. He needed me to help him build it back up. So I would leave at about 11:30 and be up to the Little Store about 1:30 a.m. and work, and it didn't take long to build it back up. One day a customer was with Sal and me, and I forget what had happened, but he said, "Sal, I'd fire Bob." I said, "Sal can't fire me." And he said, "Why not?" And I said, "He never hired me. He just called me and said I had to help him, so he never hired me, so he can't fire me, so there."

# The 1980s

After a while running back up to West Chester somehow I got started peddling produce. I started out hauling for stands in Delaware, then started getting stops in Pennsylvania, and on and on until I had a route built up, and that lasted through September. Then Sal would call and say, "Hey, Bob," I would go up to bake for the winter, and this went on for years. In the summer I would be doing produce, and I would have something tell me to stop at the Little Store because they needed me, and when I walked through the door, Louise, Sal's wife would say, "Thank God, we prayed, and here you are." They needed me to do something special. Over several years this happened at different times.

What used to make me feel good was that Sal would have somebody work in the summer, and I would go back in the fall. I would put things in the case, and in the morning people came, and they would look and say, "Hurray, Bob's back," and somebody said, "How do you know?" And they would say, "Just look at the Danish and sticky buns. Only Bob makes them like that."

One time I messed with Sal. I was picking blueberries, and that morning I made 12 dozen blueberry muffins. Sal saw all the muffins and said, "What's this?" I said, "Sorry, Sal.

I thought I hadn't made the muffins, and I got carried away. We can put some in the freezer if we don't need them until tomorrow, but we'll see." He didn't know I used fresh blueberries, but he found out in a hurry. A lady bought one and bit into it and said, loudly, "These are fresh blueberries." Everybody grabbed muffins, and Sal came back and said, "You think you're smart, don't you?" And I said, "What are you talking about?" And he said, "You know what you did. And you knew they would sell." All 12 dozen were gone in two hours.

Probably about two more years I stayed with Sal at the Little Store. Then I moved on, for my wife had some money, and we rented a place in Upper Parkeford, and set up a produce stand with flowers.

I had a produce route going for myself, and Sally wanted to help, so we did the stand, and guess what? She went out and bought a 24-foot camper, which we put up at Parkeford to stay there. She had a job at the prison in Smyrna and came up on weekends.

I had, at the time, four Genardi's stores. I hauled corn, tomatoes, and cantaloupes in to them seven days a week. One day, Jim from Genardi's asked me if I could get flowers for the stores, and I said I could, and started getting flowers for them. The big guys didn't want to sell to them unless they took a lot, and that changed after I got the stores built up. The big boys moved and took over the flower business. But that was alright, for I was just a nickel and dime. So be it. I survived.

Bob Spaz, of Spaz Beverage, said one day that I could set up on his corner and sell corn, which I did. It took off and worked out for one season, but then the township didn't want me there. I sold corn, tomatoes, and cantaloupes there. This one day, an older lady came by, and she was picking up my tomatoes and squeezing them. I watched for a minute or two, and she kept it up. I said, "Lady, these are ripe." And she said, "I want ripe tomatoes." I said, "These are ready to eat now." She kept squeezing my tomatoes. Then I got upset and said, "Lady, how would you like me to grab your butt like you are grabbing my tomatoes?" And next thing, she put four tomatoes on the scale and paid me and left. There were six or seven women there and they laughed for you have to know me to appreciate me, and one said, "She deserved that." The lady came back about ten days later, and I apologized to her for being rude. She said she was wrong and I needed to stop her before I did. I would have, and she said, "I laughed all the way home. I like you. You're alright in my book." About that time, a lady was picking up tomatoes, and she told her, "Don't squeeze the tomatoes." We laughed, and she came back every week.

When I first started with Genardi's, I dealt with Ray Tag, who was head buyer in the produce department. Bob Scotti was produce manager in Exton. Bob and I hit it off right away, for I was hauling fresh corn, lopes, and tomatoes every day as needed. As always, I believed in guaranteeing everything I sold. Once in a while, something might cost you, but that was alright, and they liked that, and they also found I was a man of my word. My word is and always is my bond. I will always remember Bob Scotti, Bob Geary, and Ritch, and I guess I forgot the others, for I dealt with six stores. After a while, Bob Scotti moved to the Goshen store and became manager there, and Bob Geary was in Exton.

After dealing with Genardi's for a while, Carol Heacock was the flower girl at Goshen, and one day asked if I could do flowers, and I said yes.

My day in the summer started at 2:00 a.m., and I would get back home at 10:00 p.m. This was seven days a week in produce season.

I also had a few other stops. John Merion was a partner in the I.G.A. in West Chester, PA, and I hauled him corn, tomatoes, lopes, melons, peppers, broccoli, peaches, apples, and other things, plus flowers. I delivered to Schedel's in Malvern, and the Little Store, and also dealt with Sam Guiantoe in West Chester, who had a wholesale route.

With all of this, I found time to go pick blueberries when in season. One year I, by myself, picked 12 to 13 pounds of blueberries, which I believe Andy said was the record for a single person to pick at his place. It was outside of Marydel, MD. One night at home my wife said, "You messed up today." And I said, "How?" She said, "I found a stem." I picked clean blueberries, and Andy used to say, "I'll trade you berries," for his weren't that clean. He said, "I don't know how you pick like that. Nobody picks that clean." One day, while out picking berries, I had two buckets full and had them setting in the shade under a bush. I heard a noise and there was a bird on the side of the bucket, and I said, "Go get your own berries," and it flew away.

In the early part of the season, we didn't get corn until the back end of June, so if you were wondering how I got everything done, it was that I would get done delivering early, go home, and cook supper, then go out and pick blueberries until dark. Andy let me do that as long as I was back where nobody could see me. When I got done picking, I would take them home and pint them up, and put them into flats for the markets. John Merion had the I.G.A. in West Chester, PA, for years until he moved on, and then he opened up a place called the

Produce Hut on Route 1 in Concordville. He's still there doing produce and other things. I, at one time, hauled him a lot of flowers, but that is all in the past. We have too many places selling flowers anymore, so John sticks to what he knows best. John does a good job. He keeps good, fresh produce and has friendly high school girls working afternoons, and he has Mo, an older lady, working days, along with Laraine, and John's wife works some, too. John is open all year, and only closes for Thanksgiving and Christmas.

Donald Hale had a big farm in Salisbury, MD, and he grew lopes that weighed as high as 18 pounds and were the best lopes at the market. When I started hauling them into Genuardi's, I sold to them by the piece, and they weighed some and said, "We're going to sell them by the pound." They made a killing, and they loved me, and said, "Bob, you are the best wholesaler we have." I said, "What about all the big guys?"

*Produce Hut*

And they said, "We don't care. You are the best in our book. Nobody does things like you. Nobody. You are the best." That made me feel really good to know they watched and saw what I used to do when I was in their stores, and also I would find things for them. I was the only supplier that, when the back door was locked at 2 p.m., they let me come in the front door any time that they were open.

I always seemed to be able to gauge what a store was selling corn-wise, and I was pretty good at putting the right amount of corn in each store. But one Sunday morning, I had 1,500 ears for Exton, and when I went into the cooler, there were still 4 carts of corn in there, so I couldn't justify putting 1,500 more in there. So I went back out into the store and saw where the corn should be, and it was empty. There were two boys who worked on weekends, and I said to them, "You need to put corn up." They said, "We will get to it later." That wasn't good enough for me, so I went and pulled two carts out and put them up. I also saw they hadn't filled the strawberries, so I went back and got some flats out and put them up. Now it was close to the time church was letting out, so I brought the other two carts out and set them in front of the other corn and helped put some other produce up, and here comes the church crowd, and the two carts of corn were gone, and now I could put the 1,500 ears in the cooler.

Chesterbrook was my last stop every day, and after I took off what they ordered, I would sometimes have corn and lopes left over, so I would give Bob Geary, who was produce manager, the rest of what I had so I could go home empty. One day, Joe Genuardi saw me and said, "Hey, Bob, how about sharing what you give Bob Geary with the other stores, for Bob Geary shows a better percentage than the other stores?" I said, "I'll try." One thing, I always try to take care of my customers, no matter how small or big they are—I always have and always will. My wife, God love her, used to say to me, "Why is it, when somebody calls, you have to take care of them the same day?" And I told her, "That's good business, and also, that's the way I am. I try to be better than the others."

My day in the summertime, after the corn was on, and the tomatoes and lopes, I would start out at 2:00 a.m. and go to Salisbury to Donald Hale's farm, load tomatoes and lopes, then back up to Middletown, Delaware, to unload lopes and tomatoes at Money's Market and pick up corn there, then up the road to deliver and back home by 9:00 or 10:00 at night. I did that seven days a week until the corn was done in September.

Leland Money owned Money's Market, and he had a 200-acre farm on which he grew corn for wholesale. He also

*Money's Farm Market*

had a big stand and a cheese shop. Dick was his son, who pretty well ran the farm, and Jan, Dick's wife, pretty well took care of inside, along with Leland. He was a good man, and we became friends, and I did a lot of business with him. Jan was a hell of a worker around there. I know for she used to help me unload in the morning, while waiting for corn. I am also a man who watches and observes people, and Jan was a hard worker. I took notice and also thought she was a wonderful lady.

Dick and Jan had two sons, Ricky and Mike, they were good boys and both worked on the farm. Here's a humorous story that happened, but Dick didn't think so at first. I watched Jan for some time, and she worked hard. Dick was always working on the farm, and never went when something was going on with her parents or family, Jan always took the boys, but Dick never took time off to go anywhere. One September, Jan's birthday was the second of September, and I sent her two dozen red roses, and when I got there that morning, Dick came over and said, "What the hell do you think you are doing? Are you trying to steal my wife, sending her red roses? Do you know what red roses mean? True love." I quickly said, "What? Are you kidding me? If I knew that, I would have been giving my wife yellow roses!" That broke the ice with him, and he said, "She can keep them, then." And then he was alright. Leland was back there laughing, for he knew where I was coming from. With my wife, I didn't need to have a holiday of any kind. If I saw something nice, and I thought she would like it, I would get it for her, for I loved her and always will.

There are a few more stories I have at Money's Market. One day, I forget the lady's name, but anyway, she was fixing some baskets of apples, and she was bent over, and Nightmite, the black lab, walked over and stuck her nose on her butt, and she hollered, "Bob!" I said, "Don't you know the difference between a nose and a hand?" It was a good thing Dick and the others were there for my defense, and everybody laughed.

Then there was a new boy trying to make a name for himself, I guess. He was with the Weights and Measures Division of the State of Delaware. He had a guard who carried a gun with him. I don't know why, but he did, he had checked the scale and told Jan she didn't have any tare in her scale. Jan put a piece of plastic on the scale, and it did nothing. Jan said that when she scales cheese or anything, she takes off a nickel, and he said, "If you don't have tare in it next time, I will fine you $1,500.00." I said, "What are you, some kind of nut?" He said, "Who are you?" I said, "Could be your worst nightmare." I looked at the guy with the gun on his side, and he put his hand on it, and I said, "Bad idea. You pull that out, and you will be dead, trust me." The other boy looked and said, "Don't." Good thinking, for he didn't know me. I have taken down men who pointed a gun at me seven times before. In fact, they all wound up dead. If a man points a gun at me, he better be ready to use it, or he will be dead. I don't play with guns, but have been known to kill before and I don't have a problem with it I have killed but also have saved 22 lives in burning buildings in my day.

I am also prepared to die fighting for what I believe. One day, Leland and I, were watching Dick working on the sprayer on the tractor, when a line broke and spilled some spray on the ground. There was a man from the state who had walked up and said, "I could fine you $1,500.00 for that spill. I said, "He couldn't help that the hose broke." He said, "I don't care." And I said, "Really, you don't care. You have got to be glad Leland owns this farm." And he said, "Or what?" And I said, "You would be dead right now, trust me." Then he left.

One day weeks later I had an early day, so I stopped back to drop off the baskets that I hauled corn in, and Dick said, "Bob, I love you." I said, "What's that all about?" And Dick said, "That kid for the state came in and asked if that crazy man was here, and I thought real quick and said, 'He's in the cooler. He'll be right out.' And the kid turned around and left. That's why I said that." We laughed about that.

One time Leland and his wife went up around Bar Harbor, Maine, for two weeks. I found a real estate sign with a "Sold" on it, and the night before they came home, I put it on their front lawn. Leland said to me, "How much did you get for me?" I said, "You think I did that?" And Leland said, "I know you did." We laughed about it, for we were doing something to one another from time to time.

Another time I got done early for some reason, and stopped in Money's, and Leland said, "Bob I have a man up in Long Island who said he would take up to 10,000 ears of corn if I had a way to get it to him." I had a 1983 Ford van with a 460 engine in it and 12-ply tires so I could haul weight. I said, "Is the corn picked?" Leland said, "Yes, for some reason they picked too much today, so can you haul it for me?" I said, "I'll have to get in and stack it just so. Let's see how much we can get in."

The final count when I got done was 9,500 ears of corn, He gave me directions and the address, and off I went. I got in there about 5:00, and the man was dealing with Acme at the time. He had little boxes that we could only get 25 ears in, so it turned out that by the time we got done it was near 8:00 p.m., I got home at roughly 12:00 a.m. to get a two-hour nap, then I was off and running for another day.

In the a.m., I went to Salisbury, MD, then back to Middletown, DE, to unload part of my load, load corn, and then into PA, and back home by 9:00 to 10:00 p.m. One night I was talking to Don Hale, and I heard my wife say, "We are like mushrooms. They keep us in the dark and feed us crap." I told Don what she said, and we had to laugh, for the way we worked, we needed a laugh once in a while.

One day there was a big storm in Middletown, and it tore a roof off of one of Leland's sheds. He got the metal sheets to cover the roof, but his men were afraid to walk on the nailers, for they thought they would fall through the nailers, and Leland said, "Now what am I to do? I guess I'll have to find a carpenter to do the job." I said, "I am waiting for the men to pick my corn, so I can do what you need. I used to put roofs on years ago, and you don't forget."

Leland said, "You'll do that?" I said, "Stop talking, and get a couple men to shove the sheets up to me, and I'll top nail the sheets, and when I get the roof covered, they can finish nailing them." Leland said, "Bob, you are a life saver. Thanks." I said, "No problem. What are friends for if we can't help one another?"

# The 1990s & 2000s

I hauled corn, tomatoes, and lopes for years, and I said, "When the bushel of corn feels like 100 pounds, that's when I will quit." 1999 was that year, but I still hauled tomatoes and lopes.

Backing up a bit, what I need to address is my wife. Back in 1992, she was operated on for breast cancer, and it took place on my birthday, which is March 18th. She had to go through radiation and chemo. I took her every day for chemo.

Four and a half years later, she had another operation again on my birthday, this time for lung cancer. They took part of a lung, and she had to go through radiation and chemo again. She got over that, but she was working in the office at the Smyrna State Prison and finally had to take medical leave and retired, for she couldn't work anymore. I spent as much time as I could with her, and took her places she liked, for we knew she was on borrowed time, and I wanted her to live some. She wanted to go back to Myrtle Beach one more time, and we did. We used to go to Longwood Gardens in the spring and at Christmastime we had friends that went with us, John and Florence W., who had variety stores years before and had to go bankrupt on account of the big stores. Sad, but it happened.

She liked to go to the zoo in Philadelphia each year, and the last year we went, there was a cow at the zoo. Sally and I were standing there by the cow, and a teacher had a class that looked like third grade-age, and my wife said, "Behave yourself." I said, "What are you talking about?" And she said, "You know what I mean." Then I reached over and squirted a boy in the eye with milk, and she said, "I knew it." The teacher turned and said, "You must be a farmer." I said, "Yes."

We lived in Hartly, DE, for years, and she liked to go to Paoli, in PA, to church every Sunday, and I was always working at something. One day, Sally started getting worse, and we went to the cancer doctor. There was a new doctor who came in from Ohio and he went over her x-rays and told us that he spotted that she had cancer starting in her bones. Nobody picked up on it before that. He sent us to a specialist, and he looked at her x-rays, and said it was too late for him to be able to do anything. The only thing he told her was to get a neck brace, and that was it. She wore this as long as she lived.

She was still going to church, and one Sunday she came home crying, for she had an accident. The Wessamans brought her home, and I had the car towed to a garage. I told her to just relax and rest. But she said she wouldn't be able to go to church, and I said, "You will." But she said, "You are always working." And I said, "Work is done for now." And every week I took her back up for church. From that day forward I stayed with her and took care of her 24 hours a day from then until one day, after several months of taking care of my girl, she was getting worse, but she was still going with my help. Her last weeks I had to carry her everywhere, from the bed to the bathroom to the living room and to the kitchen, and up to her last week at home I took her to church. Her last week at home, she said, "You can't go on like this." I said, "Whatever it takes, I'll do." But she said, "I have to go to the hospital. I mean it now, and I'll call 911." So I took her to Christiana Hospital, and she was there for five days. I stayed with her as long as I could, and John and Florence would be there when I wasn't. We kept relieving one another for five days. It was March 15, 2000, when she died. I had a viewing in Smyrna on the 18th, which was my birthday, and we took her back to Paoli for her funeral on Monday. She is buried in Philadelphia Memorial Park, God love her, as I do always. Somebody asked how long we were married, and I said, "She put up with me for 45 years, and we were hoping to get to 50 years, but we didn't make it." I had the service in the church she loved so much, where we used to go years ago. Her classmates were there in numbers, and our vet, Dr. William Weicket cancelled appointments to come to her funeral. Dr. Weichelt is head of the West Chester Animal Emergency Center and is a well-respected veterinarian. He was even presented in 2010 with a Lifetime Achievement Award by the Pennsylvania Veterinary Medical Association. Cancelling those appointments says a lot about what he thought of her, and me, for he took care of our dogs. Talking about dogs, four went in the casket with Sally to keep her company. There were about 200 people who showed up to her service, which makes you feel good if you can.

After we lost Abbey, our fourth cocker spaniel, we went a few weeks, and Sally had asked Willie about another cocker. He had a name of someone in New Jersey that had a litter of pups. At the time, before we had Abbey, we had Ginger and Joy. So I said, with Sally's cancer, as we were going over the bridge to NJ, "No way in hell are we bringing two dogs home."

We got over to the place, and she had two pups left. We were playing with them, and I looked at Sally and started laughing. The lady wanted $600.00 per dog, but she said, if we took both we could have them for $1,000.00. We had money back from taxes, so the lady said, "Is there something I missed?" I told her I had said we weren't going home with two dogs, but I guess we were now. I was glad, for they gave Sally a lot of happiness before she left us. It was a bad time for me, but the pups helped out.

In 2001, I had my hip replaced in Kent General Hospital in Dover, DE. Dr. Lawrence Piccion did the operation, and three days later my brother and his wife were down from PA. I guess it was a dietician who came in and wanted to ask me how the food was, and my brother said, "He is going to tell you, and you won't like it, trust me. I know him. He says what he thinks." She asked about the food, and I told her, "It's not your fault, for you have the head people buy the cheapest food they can buy, so you can't do much with that." She walked out of the room. The doctor came in and asked what rehab I would be doing and I said, "I'm going home. Got a problem with that? I don't have time to be sick."

The Tuckers took care of the dogs while I was in the hospital. Jim, Lydia, Joshua, and Jeremy Tucker would come over to help me for a while, until I got up and running again. A nurse and a therapy boy came to the house for a week, and he said, "When you start driving I can't come anymore." Ten days after I came home, I was hauling watermelons and lopes from MD to Dover. Then in a few more days I was back hauling tomatoes and lopes, plus the charcoal. And guess what? I started getting equipment together, for I was going back to doing what I knew best—baking.

*(My wife gave this to me. It is what she thought of me.)*

That man
Is a Success

Who has lived well,
Laughed often, and loved much

Who has gained the respect
Of intelligent men
And the love of children

Who has filled his niche
And accomplished his task
Who leaves the world better
Than he found it
Whether by an improved poppy
Or a rescued soul

Who looked for the best in others
And gave the best he had

I set up an oven and mixing and donut fryer, baking table, racks, and pans. I started back to baking my sticky buns and Danish and pies and cakes. I did three wedding cakes and several birthday cakes. I started hauling back up to PA and got stops. I started with Produce Hut and Westtown Meat, and Worrell's Butcher Shop, plus a few other stops. I also had some stops in Delaware, and I also had hauled produce off of T.A. Farms a while back, and somehow I had got up with Dan Palmer and started making pies and sticky buns for

*Bob and Sally, 1973*

Thanksgiving and Christmas. I initially did it for his mother and dad in 2002, then in 2003 I did 150 dozen sticky buns and 250 pies.

Here is something I have to go on record and tell. I used to have five stops in PA at the time, and you have to believe, for this happened, and I love telling it. I would be going up the road, and it would be raining, and about 10 minutes before I got to a stop, I would ask God to slow down the rain for 20 minutes so I could unload my baked goods, and when I pulled up, it stopped raining for a while. When I got back on the road, it started up again, and when I was just about to Westtown Meat, I asked again, and the rain stopped long enough for me to unload there. Then back on the road and the rain started again. I got to West Chester, and it stopped again. Then on to Malvern in the rain, and it stopped again for me at Worrell's Butcher Shop, and started again after I left there. That's why my faith in God is real, and I'm glad I have God in my life, praise the Lord. I believe in living my life with God and keep showing it, and people will take notice at that.

When tomatoes came in, I still hauled tomatoes to Hershey's Market and also Highland Orchards. This was 2004, and doing the baking and hauling tomatoes kept me busy. Coming into the fall there were 250 dozen sticky buns ordered and 900 pies for Thanksgiving, but that wasn't to happen, for on the fourth of November, Jerry my neighbor, and I were delivering pies and sticky buns, and thank God Jerry was with me, for I got sick at Worrell's. I could set down or lay down, and John Worrell said, "Bob you've got to go to the hospital." I said, "John, all I want is to go home." John said, "No way." The next thing I heard the ambulance pull up, and it took me to Paoli Hospital,. The next thing that I remember, they were running me into the operating room, and the doctor, who was Dr. Robert Fried said to me, "If I don't have you operated on in 10 minutes, you will be dead." I looked up at him and said, in a calm voice, "Doctor, don't worry, God is one your side, and mine, too, so He has us covered."

Three days later, with all the tubes in me, he came and sat with me and told me I was lucky, for only 20% come off the table alive. Then I asked him if he remembered what I had said, and he said, "I'll never forget it. You shook me up with that comment. You changed my life."

Jerry stayed right there with me all that time. God bless him, for they are more than friends. Jerry, Wendy, and Jerry Jr. are part of my family, God bless them. I was in the hospital for 15 days, but I had something happen the third night. There was another person in the room, and I had asked him to turn off his TV, since it was after 11:00 p.m., and he turned it up instead. About 3:00 I woke up to a crash. All my things that were on my tray were all over the floor, and I didn't know what had happened. I got out of bed, took all the tubes out of myself, got dressed, left the hospital, and headed toward the Frazier Diner at 3:30 a.m. The police found me walking on Route 30 and took me back to the hospital where Dr. Fried was waiting, and he said, "What did you do?" I passed out. They put me in a private room, and he came in in the morning, and told me I was a lucky man, taking all those tubes out. They took good care of me, and the food was great, and 15 days later, Earl, my brother, was there, and Dr. Fried came in and asked, "What rehab do you want to go to?" I said, "Home." He said, "No way with what you went through." And Earl said, "Doc, it's no use going that route, 'cause you won't win. You don't know him. He is somebody you don't argue with, trust me on this one. He is going home and nobody will stop him, for here comes his ride now, so get the paperwork ready." The doctor said, "Okay, but you'd better not work for a couple of weeks, and then don't lift over 25 pounds for at least 6 months." Jerry said, "Yeah, right, he's going to listen." And Earl said, "That will be the day."

Jerry took me home, and a nurse came to the house to check the dressings and asked, "Who does the cooking?" I said, "I do. What do you think I am, an invalid? I am not, and after this week, I won't need you. I can do for myself." She came two more times, and that was it. Four days later, I was back working. Back at the hospital, after about three days, I told or asked Jerry to call T.A. Farms and tell them what happened so they could call or do something about their pies. Dan worked it out with some Amish ladies to do his pies, and Jerry, Wendy, and Jim came to my rescue, to help me make 250 dozen sticky buns. Jim said, "You can't keep a good man down." And I said and always will say, "I don't have time to be sick," and kept on going.

I started back in early 2004 selling sticky buns to Glen Willow Orchard. They started out one day with about 24 packs of buns, and called me for 30 the next day and 40 the next day and every day until I got sick. Then they found someone else after that. It was a good run until I got sick. What happened was an ulcer broke in my stomach, and the hernia broke, which could kill you, and they punctured my stomach, and it went up behind my heart, and that got serious. So I got lucky. God was watching over me again.

After all of this, I got back into pedaling flowers again. Bob Quillen had a hardware store in Dover or outside of there, and I had some others, too, and one day a hardware salesman came to me and asked me if I could help Felton Hardware store out with flowers, so I went down and met Leon at the hardware and started him off with flowers, for I am and always will be for the little guys, the mom and pop stores, so to speak. They are what built the country we live in, not the big stores. The first year I sold Felton Hardware flowers, they only did 38 flats of bedding plants. We built that up until, in later years, when Rod, the son, took over, we were over a 1,000 flats and a lot of hanging baskets and big pots. He is still going, for I got him hooked up with my growers Mike Bradway at Bradway's Market and Greenhouse in Quinton, NJ, and Carmen LaRosa in Woodstown, NJ. Over the years I have done a lot of business with Carmen, and I can call him a friend. He was and still is one of the better flower growers around the country, and I mean that. "God Bless" him. I also did business with John and Mike Bradway for a while, until I had my heart attack and went down. That came later. I also have to mention a good grower from the past was Bob Wiches in Smyrna and also Maria Bobola of Dover. Also have to mention Lee Hutcheson of

*Rod Felton Hardware*

Hutcheson's Hardware in Ridgley, MD. They were nice people to work with it was a pleasure doing business with them. I also worked with Dave Hartly Hardware. I sold him Charcoal, flowers, and my sticky buns. Dave was and is a good-hearted soul and tries to help people. I was sorry I had to cut everything short, but when you go down, there's not much you can do. It was a sad day for me. I was used to working 16-18 hours a day. One day in September in 2005, my sister-in-law called me and asked me if I could go up to a place called Sharon's Sweet Beginnings and talk to her. So one day while I was in PA, I stopped in to talk to her. She said, "May I help you?" And I said, "No, I am here to maybe help you." And she said, "You are?" I said, "I am Bob Reese." The look on her face was priceless. "Oh my God," she said. "Am I glad to meet you, and thanks for coming. Edna called you, didn't she?" I said, "Yes." I talked with her that day and told her I had been looking for the right person to start up with and give them my recipes, too. So we talked, and I left that day but, came back again and talked some more, to make up my mind if she had what I was looking for, and at the time, she was ambitious, and I saw that in her. So I went back a third time and sat down with her and said, "I am going to give you my recipes." She asked, "How much is this going to cost me, for I have very little money?" I played with her and said, "A lot, but we might be able to work it out over time." She said, "I would need a lot of time." And I am laughing inside, for I am not charging her anything. I said, "Now I am going to be honest with you. What it will cost you is that when you are ready to retire or quit, you have to find somebody worthy of the recipes and give them to another person. That's it." She said, "You are kidding." I said, "No, I'm not. That's all you have to do." She said, "Thank you, thank you, Bob. I'll make you proud." Shortly after that, I was standing outside the store, and Mike from the pizza shop came out and saw me and said, "Bob, is that you?" And I said, "Yes." We talked, for Gabe owned the shop for years, and Mike was his nephew, and had it now, and about that time, Sharon came out and looked and said, "You know Mike?" And I said, "We go way back." Then Mike looked and said, "You know Bob?" Sharon said, "Yes. He's giving me his recipes and is going to help and show me how make do his recipes."

Then Mike told Sharon, "If you get half as good as Bob, you will do good, trust me, for he is the best and has been for a long time." Sharon was ready to learn, and every Monday for several weeks she came down to Hartly to work with me and learn how to roll dough and make sticky buns and Danish. I showed her how to do bread and rolls, but that didn't work out too well, for I do everything by hand.

Backing up a bit again, in 1997 I was doing business with Greg at Paoli Hardware, and they built a place at the corner of Boot Road and old Route 202. I got Greg into selling tomatoes, corn, and lopes there at the store. A while later, they closed the store, and he went back to Paoli with his dad and other brother, and he said I could set up there if I wanted to, so I started selling flowers and produce there. When I wasn't there, I had two girls helping, and soon the one left. Then Cathy Davies ran the place. She had her two Boxers, Otis and Ruby, and we got along great. Cathy was a great worker and honest, for in that kind of work you need somebody that you could trust. I guess we were there most of that summer. Then they sold that place, and they built a drugstore there.

Now back to Sharon and how we got together. Like I said, she would come down on Mondays, and when I was up

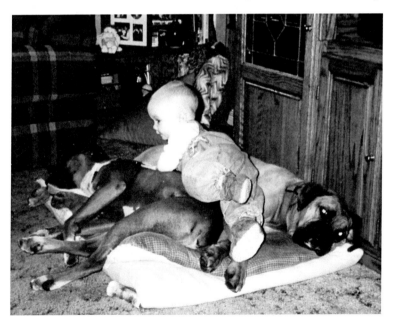

*Otis and Ruby*

in PA, I would stop and check in with her and see if there was anything I could do for her, and after a while she would call and ask me to do things or if I knew where to get supplies, and I told her my suppliers and helped her where I could. I still was doing my pies and sticky buns, charcoal, flowers, and still hauling tomatoes. Sharon said, "How do you do all of that?" I said, "You get up and get it done."

I found around the corner and down the road was a new greenhouse, so I stopped in, and a man came out. Stan Swanson was his name. I asked him if he did wholesale. He said, "Funny you stopped, for I was going out to see where I could sell some flowers." I said, "You don't have any customers?" And he said, "No." I could not believe somebody would spend $300,000.00 and start growing flowers with no customers. I said, "I'll try to peddle as much as I can for you." I started selling his flowers. He got busy, and one day he said, "I need a helper." Jeremy Tucker was looking for a job, and I told Stan, "I'll send you over a good boy." I told Jeremy about it, and he said he would go over, but he did not go right away. I would stop and ask, "Did you get the job?" And he would say, "I didn't go yet." This went on for a couple of weeks, and Stan said, "I need him. See if he still wants the job." So I got on the phone. I said, "Jeremy you better get over to see Stan, or I'll be over there and boot you all the way there." That got him moving, and afterwards he thanked me for making him go. We laughed because he said, "I believed you would have booted me, too." They got along real good. Jeremy turned out to be a good worker and has done well for himself.

Now back to Sharon and her journey with me helping when I could with whatever she needed from me. She had started or actually bought out a candy and supply store a while before I showed up, and there was a piece in the local news about her and her shop. Somehow I was mentioned in the article as an old baker, which I was, but she had me like I was an old man. I am 83 and still going on and working and helping Sharon out.

When Sharon was coming down on Mondays, she found one of my formula books and found more recipes and was copying them out of my book, which was okay. Before this, I set up my brother's bakery in Engleside Diner and left my recipes there for Earl to use, and I guess you can say it came back to bite me in the butt. For after Sharon got my recipes and started using some, she told everybody she had Engleside Diner's recipes, but they were mine, and I told her so, She told me Engleside Diner was well-known and I wasn't. But she didn't know I had been known all over the country, for I used to ship my sticky buns all over the country, and I shipped to the White House back in the '70s. They came to me, not me to them.

I put up with some of the things she does and says, for she is my beautiful daughter, and I love her to death. We get along fairly well, but she can be stubborn, and hard-headed like me. We do get into arguments once in a while, then get over it.

I had helped her with cakes, and I did the pastries and pies, but a few years ago I couldn't ice the cakes anymore, which hurt me, for I worked hard and long hours all my life. But I realized I couldn't do what I was able to do for years.

My brother, Earl, called me one day, I believe in 2009, and asked if I knew anything about the memorial plaque that was made and put up in the corner of Larry Polite's cornfield in 1943 until it disappeared. I said I thought it was up in Harold Martin's barn. So I went looking and asking around, but no-

*Exton Post Office Dedication, 1964*

*WWII Memorial, Exton*

*WWII Names on Memorial, Exton*

## Program: Unveiling and Dedication of Roll of Honor
West Whiteland Township, Chester County,
January 9, 1944, 2:00 PM
Exton, Pennsylvania

*Roll of Honor (As of January 9, 1944)*

George Ashbridge, 3rd
Paul W. Bair
William Bowman
George B. Bowman
Margaret E. Campbell
George C. Chandler
Thomas A. Clark
Earl J. Cohere, Jr.
Frederick J. Coover
Thomas J. Crewdson
David A. Daly
James A. Daly
John M. Daly
Harvey G. Dawson
Robert L. Dawson
John T. Detraz
Clayton Dukeman
Homer C. Dutt
Victor E. Dutt
David L. Ehrhart, Jr.
J. Ralph Ellison
Edwin F. Erwin
Elwood D. Erwin

Charles E. Fisher
Samuel C. Fisher
James F. Fitzgerald, Jr.
Donald I. Forbes
Albert Foreman
Charles V. Gunkle
Charles Granberry
William H. Haldeman
Joseph R. Higgins
A. Myrtle Hopkins
Samuel C. Hopkins
James W. Howse, 3rd
Lewis A. Hunter
W. Lee Hunter
John Kent Kane, Jr.
Paul V. Kocker, Jr.
William F. Kellon
**Robert B. Knight
Thomas H. Lantz
Frederick F. Lewis
Harvey H. Lewis
William J. Loftus
Edmund Lucas

George C. Mahers
Louis E. Mahers
William F. Mahers
Harold D. Martin
Edwin H. Messner
Thomas M. McIlvaine
William R. McIlvaine
Thomas J. Montgomery
Warren B. Moore
Francis J. Murray
William H. Murray
H. Kenton Newlin
Charles E. Nuttall
Elmer R. Nuttall
Wheeler H. Page
*William Parker
Walter C. Peck
Warren Peck
Glenn R. Plank
Earl H. Reese

Clyde E. Reese, Jr.
Alexander Rush
Benjamin Rush, 3rd
Anthony Rossi
William H. Schiebe
Harwood A. Schuyler
Charles V. Shreiner, Jr.
Charles F. Simcox
Walter P. Smith
Laird R. Snowden
David Street
Horace G. Thomas
Clifton D. Walton
Joshua B. Walton
George A. Waters
Harriet M. Yerkes
Leicester A. Yerkes
John R. Young
Robert E. Young

---

*\*\* Killed in action*
*\* Missing in action*

body knew anything about it. Earl was in the *Daily Local* with a piece about looking for it and asking anybody to call him, but to no avail. I told him that one day, when I made enough money, I would see that it got remade and put up again.

It is a shame the township won't do anything about it. I guess they don't care about the past and the people that helped build this country. One of these days, somebody in the township better get off their ass and do something about replacing this memorial for the men and women who went to war in the Second World War. You in the government should be ashamed of yourself for this.

I also want to get a picture of my mother, to be put up in the Exton Post Office, for she was and probably will be for a long time, the only 30-year Postmaster at the Exton Post Office. She started in 1936 and retired in 1966. We had the post office in our restaurant from 1966 until 1973, I think, and then they built a new post office on Route 30 in Exton. That is when they started with a mail carrier.

Now I will go back at this time and sort of reminisce about my past and people I've done business with over the years that I had become close to, starting with William H. Murray and his brother, Franny. Bill had the appliance store in Paoli, and I always remember Franny. He had school buses and was always asking me to drive for him, and I said, "Franny, you don't have enough money for me to drive a school bus. No way you will get me to drive."

Then there was John and Florence Wassam. I sold them charcoal in the '60s, at their Wassam's Variety Stores in Delaware, and they are still good friends of mine. They were by my side in the last years of my wife and with me to her death. God bless them. I'll always be grateful for them, and they are still there for me.

There was a place called the Farm Market on Route 100, and Max Morris had it built in the late '40s. Felix Presto took over from Max, and I sold him Charcoal, ice, and produce. We are still friends today.

Then there is David and his wife at Marchwood Hardware. I sold charcoal to him for years, and he is still in business withstanding the big stores. People today don't seem to care about the mom and pop stores that built this country which is a shame. Spaz beverage is another. I still am friends with Bob Spaz and his dad. Bob was a great friend and a good man. Bill Lamb, of Lamb Beverage, and I were good friends, and Tex Reynolds worked for Lamb Beverage for years. That's where my middle name Austin came from. Then there was Larry Polite, who had the Guernsey cow across the road from our place. We had a restaurant, gas station, and Mom had the post office.

Then there was Ernie and his wife, who had a store down on Route 30. Henry Smith had the garage, and that is where we used to pitch quays on Saturday nights. Harold Martin had the Exton Lodge, and Domick Pollite and Joe Mena had the Exton Diner, which they started in 1948.

Now Tony, Domick's son, has the Frazier Diner in Frazier, PA, and does a nice job. He was also a friend for years, but he might say different. We are always kidding one another. Then there is John Merion, who had the I.G.A. in West Chester in the '80s and '90s, and today has what is called the Produce Hut on Route 1 in Concordville, PA. He sells all fresh fruit and produce. Stop in when that way and say hello. Also, Penny and Jerry at the Westtown Meat on 202 south of West Chester. They are good people and have been there for many years and do a good job. They sell my chocolate pretzels and sticky buns, which I am famous for. And then there is also John

*Felix Presto*

*Jay Presto,
Felix's Market*

*Felix's Market*

Worrell of Worrell Butcher Shop in Malvern, PA, who deals in high-end meats, and does soups and dishes for people to take home to pop in the microwave. He also sells my charcoal, and we have been friends a long time. In fact, he saved my life in '94 by making me go to the hospital. I sold John charcoal and used to sell him sticky buns and pies, but sales were off, so I stopped taking things there.

Still in Malvern, I did work for Gus Rubino, who has Rubino's TV Repair in Malvern, and is also a friend of mine for years, and I used to put up antenna for him years ago.

Back in Delaware, I lived in Hartly for 21 years and did business with Dave Brown, who owns the Hartly Hardware Store. He sold my sticky buns, charcoal, and flowers. Dave had a fire, and it is taking him a long time to get back open, but he will make it soon.

I used to buy flowers and pick strawberries at Bobola Florist and Farm. They are a family farm worked by Ted and Maria Bobola and their two sons. They also have chicken houses, and they all work on the farm and do a good job.

Down in Felton I do business with Felton Hardware. Rod and his dad have run the hardware store since 1964, and this shows you there are still family businesses operating.

I also did business with Flaskey's in Middletown, and they are another family farm. John and Cindy, plus their son and daughter work the farm together. Family farms are what made this country, not the big corporations, and thank God they will never get rid of the family farms, for they are a good breed of people and are hard workers, and that is something the younger don't know anything about.

I myself always worked 16 hours a day and a lot of times more.

Years ago I started working with Donald Hales, and a few months went by, when he said, "I thought I was the only crazy guy, but I found another one."

Then there was Ed Powell up by Blackbird, and he farmed and also raised raspberries and blackberries, and for years I helped pick and deliver for him.

Over in NJ, I did business with Bradway's Market and Greenhouse, Mike, the son, and John, his father. I hauled flowers from there, and also bought flowers from Carmen LaRosa in Woodstown for years. Carmen is one of the best flower growers around the area for my money.

I also bought Indian corn from Stecker in Swedesboro, NJ, which is also a family farm. Gary and Glenn each had seven children, and they all worked on the farm. They grew vegetables and Indian corn and mums, and have a stand, too.

---

Now back to my girl, Sharon, and the bakery and helping her at times while I was still doing baking in Delaware for myself. Sharon would call me to go pick things up at times. I was always on the way up when she called, and she said, "How do you know?" And I would say, "God tells me."

After a couple of years, I was delivering to Worrell's, Westtown Meat, and Produce Hut, and Jerry was with me again. I was at Sharon's, and I had a lot of pain, and it wouldn't stop, so Jerry took me to Paoli Hospital again. Sharon got all upset and after a while called the hospital and asked how I was, and they said they couldn't tell her, and she said, "I am his daughter." Then they told her, I would be okay. They had to give me a shot, for my medicine wasn't working as it should have. They gave me a bigger dose. Sharon was a wreck the rest of the day. I was still hauling tomatoes and charcoal, and doing my own baking, plus helping Sharon out, too.

Years later I was in the hospital again, and Jerry drove me up from Hartly to Paoli again, and after a while they said, "You had mild heart failure." The doctor said, "You had better find a hospital closer, for you might not make it next time." But I said, "No way."

I guess it was early 2012 that Earl and Sharon were on me to move up before something bad happened. I was still living in Hartly, DE. I finally gave in one day and moved up to Sharon's. She had a one-room apartment, so I could live with her, only I had my own place, which was on the back of her house, so she could keep an eye on me and take care of me somewhat. Two weeks from the day I moved they took me to Paoli Hospital with a heart attack. I was in the emergency room with Dr. Tucci, who is a heart doctor, and Dr. Fried saw me, and said to Dr. Tucci, "You save him, for I saved him once, and I still would like some sticky buns," and laughed. Dr. Tucci got me straightened out in a few days and let me go home. I rested a couple of days, then went back to work.

Sharon had broken an engagement that lasted about ten years, for he wasn't going to marry her, and after a while went on the net and started dating different ones, which made me worry, for you never know today with the crazy ones out there. She didn't know how much I worried. I guess I am like an old mother hen when it comes to Sharon. I love her to death, and I told her one day, if it came down to it, I would give my life so she could live, in a heartbeat. I would stay up at night until she came home, which could be 2:00 a.m. or later, and I worried all the time. I love my daughter with all my heart, for she's all

I've got anymore. She finally settled down with one man for a while, and that didn't work out, and I'm glad.

I later was taken back to the hospital again. I wasn't drinking enough water, so I was there for three days then back home. About another six months went by and I had another heart attack. I was in the hospital for about a week and then back home again. Sharon wouldn't let me work for a while. When I went in after that, she would look at me, and if she thought I didn't look good, she'd tell me to go home.

Then one day, about another six months or so, I was working and I got a pain. I took a nitro and I went and sat down, and the next thing I heard Sharon calling 911 for an ambulance and off to Paoli again. After that she said, "You are not working here at night by yourself. You work when I am here from now on." I had gotten a medical alert to wear after that and had to use it one night about 7:00. The ambulance was there, and they were working on me, and Sharon came in and said, "What's going on?" The tech said, "Who are you?" And Sharon said, "He's my dad." Then they said, "He passed out again. He hit the alert, and they sent us here. He's not drinking enough water again." So now I watch that I drink enough water.

Sharon had a relationship for about five years, which ended badly. So after six months to a year back on the internet, she was dating different men, which caused me to worry about her again. I guess she didn't realize that was causing me more problems, but she kept it up anyway.

The next time I went to the hospital they did tests, for I was having trouble breathing, and they found I have COPD caused by my time fighting fires. I would run in with no mask on and bring people out of the fire, so now I am paying for a

*Bob and Sharon, in bakery*

*Bob and Sharon, 2012*

*Herb Funderwhite*

*Sally, Violet, Bob, Earl and Clyde*

good deed. I need oxygen sometimes, but they won't give it to me, so I have to stay inside with the air on. In the meantime I was having a hard time moneywise, and I stopped in one night and saw Herb Funderwhite. We were talking about old times, for I knew him for years, for he worked for John Mowner laying block, a far cry from farming, which he had done as a boy. After a while he asked what I had been doing, and I told him I had been in Delaware for years, and now was back up here for the time being but still had a place in Delaware. I told him I was having a hard time paying my bills. He asked if I need help, and I said, "I need somebody to help me."He said, "I know how you used to help people, so if you need something, I can help." Herb gave me money and said, "I don't want it back." I thanked him. I would stop and see Herb as often as I could, and he helped me some more after that. I was grateful for that, and I used to bring him blackberries from time to time. Herb would ask me to go with him for company, for he was having health problems, and I would stay with him at times.

Sharon and I we were keeping afloat at the bakery, for neither one of us was getting paid, but that didn't bother me, and I helped out however I could. Her wagon went up on her, and I had a small van and a big one, so I let her have the small van for as long as she needed it, which was several months, but I didn't mind, for I love her and would do anything for her.

Sharon told me one day I couldn't decorate cakes anymore, for I am old school, and there's more to it today. I see how everybody wants special things on their cakes, and like I told her, "Back in our day, in the '70s, you only had yellow cake and chocolate cake, that was it." It tickled me, one day she had, I believe, fifteen cakes to do, and she was complaining, and I said, "How or what would you do back in the '70s, for we did 55 birthday cakes a day, every day?" She said, "I would cry."

Now changing things, I went grocery shopping one day at Croppers. I was in line and watching the checker. There were five people ahead of me, and the checker never smiled the whole time. I got in front of her and said, "Smile, for you could be on candid camera." She gave me a big smile. Two weeks later I was there again, and three people were in front of me, and she didn't smile for them, but when I got in front of her, and without me saying anything, I got a big smile. Every time I went in, I got a smile from her, and then I didn't see her for a while, and I asked, and they said, "She's working in the bakery." So I found her in the bakery, and I stood there, and she saw me and came out to give me a hug and a big smile. Then we talked for a couple of minutes. About two weeks later, I saw her, and we talked, and I gave her my phone number and name, and she gave me hers, and she said she would be graduating from Downingtown High, and I told her we would make her a cake. Her name is Nicola.

Backing up a bit, I would go up and stay with Herb, for he was getting worse. I went most weekends, Saturday and Sunday, to keep him company, and we would go places until he couldn't go anymore. After quite a while, he had to go to the hospital, and it wasn't long before he passed on to a better place, God bless him. I'll never forget Herb. I have his picture on my dresser, so I see him every morning and night. Herb was a good man, and a dear friend, and I stay in touch with his daughters.

I also got ahead of myself, for two years before, we moved from Downingtown to Thorndale, in the back of a row of stores by Caln School. The address is 3535 Lincoln Highway

*Carnival Mask Cake*

*Castle Cake*

*Eagle Scout Cake*

*Hockey Cake*

in Thorndale, PA, 19372, phone number 610-209-3969 for anybody who would like to come, for after the book comes out, we will have a book signing at this address. All will be welcome.

I forgot to mention my doctor in Clayton, who was Robert Donnick. He was my primary doctor of record for 21 years. Now, it is Dr. Earl Fried in Lionville who, after a time I went to him, and he gave me an EKG and afterwards said to me, and I thought he was talking about my heart, but it turned out he wasn't. He said, "You know you have to be careful now, for you have been up here a while, and people are starting to know you are back, and there are still jealous husbands still looking for you," and he laughed. And I said, "I forgot how well you knew me."

Back to Sharon and me at the bakery, the last couple of years have been hard. Since the recession, business fell over about 40%, which hurts, but we are still here and hope to stay for a while yet. Sharon hasn't let me do what I would, but that will change one day. Right now she has a new man who will be in her life soon. She talks to him online, which I know nothing about and don't want to know. I am from the old school. I tell them we started out with carrier pigeons, then the party line phone, then the dial phone.

We do, or Sharon does, birthday cakes and wedding cakes, and she does a good and great job, and I am proud of her. She's my beautiful daughter. I'll be beside her until the day I die. I am 83 now. I expect to pass 100 years!

Now to finish up with a bang, here goes! Sharon has been online with a fellow talking back and forth, and one day she said, "I am going to have a date with him." He lives in Harrisburg, which is an hour and a half away from us.

She met him around Lancaster, which is halfway. The next thing I know, she went to Harrisburg to see him. Then after a few weeks, she went up and stayed the weekend. Then he came down here and stayed the weekend, and this went on for quite a while, and now she goes up there on Friday nights and comes home on Tuesday mornings in time to go to work. This has now gone on for a year, and a couple of weeks ago they set a date to get married, thank God and bless them. I guess I am going to lose her, for I guess she will move to Harrisburg for good, and I will probably only see her a couple of times a year. So, if that's the case, I might go to Florida to see and help Sal and Louise out. Before I close, I want to say a few things about Bumps and Barb Miller. I watched them grow up in Exton back in the day. Bumps worked for me when I had the beer business, and Barb worked at Gilley's Luncheonette. I was honored one day when they came to me seeking my advice, which I was happy to provide to them. For now, God bless everyone.

*Bob and Bubi*